SECULARIZATION
AND
MISSION

Christian Mission and Modern Culture

EDITED BY
ALAN NEELY, H. WAYNE PIPKIN,
AND WILBERT R. SHENK

In the Series:

SECULARIZATION
AND
MISSION

A Theological Essay

BERT HOEDEMAKER

TRINITY PRESS
INTERNATIONAL
HARRISBURG, PENNSYLVANIA

Gracewing

59871

First published by
TRINITY PRESS INTERNATIONAL
P.O. Box 1321
Harrisburg, PA 17105
U.S.A.

First British edition
published by
GRACEWING
2 Southern Avenue
Leominster
Herefordshire HR6 0QF
England

Trinity Press International is a division
of the Morehouse Group.

Scripture quotations are from the Revised Standard Version Bible, copyright 1973, Division of Christian Education of the National Council of the Churches of Christ in the United States of America, and are used by permission.

Cover design: Brian Preuss

Library of Congress Cataloging-in-Publication Data

Hoedemaker, L.A.
    Secularization and mission : a theological essay / Bert
Hoedemaker.
        p.   cm. — (Christian mission and modern culture)
    Includes bibliographical references.
    ISBN 1-56338-224-5 (alk. paper)
    1. Secularization (Theology)   2. Missions—Theory   I. Title.
II. Series.
BT83.7.H64   1998
266'.001—dc21   97-41099
                                                                CIP

Gracewing ISBN: 0-85244-481-8

Printed in the United States of America

98 99 00 01 02 6 5 4 3 2 1

Contents

Preface to the Series

Both Christian mission and modern culture, widely regarded as antagonists, are in crisis. The emergence of the modern mission movement in the early nineteenth century cannot be understood apart from the rise of technocratic society. Now, at the end of the twentieth century, both modern culture and Christian mission face an uncertain future.

One of the developments integral to modernity was the way the role of religion in culture was redefined. Whereas religion had played an authoritative role in the culture of Christendom, modern culture was highly critical of religion and increasingly secular in its assumptions. A sustained effort was made to banish religion to the backwaters of modern culture.

The decade of the 1980s witnessed further momentous developments on the geopolitical front with the collapse of communism. In the aftermath of the breakup of the system of power blocs that dominated international relations for a generation, it is clear that religion has survived even if its institutionalization has undergone deep change and its future forms are unclear. Secularism continues to oppose religion, while technology has emerged as a major source of power and authority in modern culture. Both confront Christian faith with fundamental questions.

The purpose of this series is to probe these developments from a variety of angles with a view to helping the church understand its missional responsibility to a culture in crisis. One important resource is the church's experience of two centuries of cross-cultural mission that has reshaped the church into a global Christian *ecumene*. The focus of our inquiry will be the church in modern culture. The series (1) examines modern/postmodern culture from a missional point of view; (2) develops the theological agenda that the church in modern culture must address in order to recover its own integrity; and (3) tests fresh conceptualizations of the nature and mission of the church as it engages modern culture. In other words, these volumes are intended to be a forum where conventional assumptions can be challenged and alternative formulations explored.

This series is a project authorized by the Institute of Mennonite Studies, research agency of the Associated Mennonite Biblical Seminary, and supported by a generous grant from the Pew Charitable Trusts.

Editorial Committee

ALAN NEELY
H. WAYNE PIPKIN
WILBERT R. SHENK

Introduction

In ordinary speech, "secularization" means the loss of faith that is characteristic of our modern industrial-technological societies. Many people who are deeply concerned about this loss are just as deeply convinced that a strong missionary effort is needed to counteract it. Although no one would make light of such an effort—"loss of faith" is not just a problem of unbelieving individuals but of an apparently inescapable cultural development that undermines the plausibility of faith itself—this way of approaching the problem tends to be too superficial. It overlooks the fact that the process of secularization, in whatever way it is defined, calls into question the very presuppositions that underlie much traditional speaking about religion, faith, and mission.

In other words, one cannot simply place secularization and mission over against each other, or, for that matter, simply state that modern Western culture has now become a mission field. The statement is no doubt valid in a general sense; but it calls for some serious reflection about what mission might mean when it is applied to modern culture, and what kind of rethinking of mission might be necessary when we take the implications and effects of secularization seriously.

This essay intends to contribute to this reflection. It links up with the many ways in which the ecumenical movement is seeking clarity about the meaning of such key words as *mission* and *unity* in the framework of a very complex intercultural communication. Its basic thesis is that missionary thinking needs to be reconstructed against the background of the global experience of secularization. The term *secularization* refers to the fact that the relation between religion, rationality, and faith—the basic components with which human beings "read" their world—is in disarray. The disarray stems from a typically Western problem that has been and is being globalized. This globalization creates a common culture, to a certain extent. As such it raises the question and suggests the possibility of a genuine unity of humankind, but it is obviously unable to establish it. It is at this point that the problematic situation of humankind and the traditional missionary agenda meet; they challenge each other to reinterpretation and reconstruction.

Given this thesis, it is inevitable that the phenomenon of fundamentalism is touched upon in virtually each of the six chapters. Fundamentalism is seen as a challenge to be taken very seriously in the reflection on secularization and mission. In this essay it is interpreted as an effort to seek shortcuts in the confrontation with the modern problem of religion and rationality. That is a strong temptation, and not only the specific movements usually called "fundamentalism" yield to it. The temptation competes with the opposite temptation to accept the premises of secularization as inevitable. Responsible missionary faith and missionary thinking should endeavor to avoid both pitfalls.

1

Secularization

The term *secularization* refers to a far-reaching change in the relation between religion and culture. It is often used in connection with the widespread experience that the dominant institutions of modern culture have emancipated, even alienated themselves from religion, and that, conversely, traditional religious institutions and believers have become marginal phenomena in that culture as far as their religion is concerned. Beyond this general reference, however, there is little consensus about what exactly the term means and how the process that is designated by it should be understood.

Religion and Modernity

When taken at face value, the term *secularization* presupposes that there is something like a territorial battle between religion and world, that religion is forced to yield more and more ground in that battle, and that modern culture is largely a product of this. The metaphor of territorial battle goes back to the original legal meaning of secularization as the transfer of clerical goods into worldly possession. It is the main ingredient in the so-called secularization thesis, which, under the influence of Max Weber, proclaims an ongoing rationalization of society, eventually leading to the disappearance of religion.

This secularization thesis, however, is increasingly losing support. To be sure, it can hardly be doubted that religion is losing public ground, and that traditional religious
institutions have difficulty surviving under the pressure of
purely secular fashions and lifestyles. Nevertheless, there is
no evidence of a disappearance of religion. Although the
relation between religion and public life may undergo radical change, religion as such is alive (cf. Hammond 1985;
also Hadden and Shupe 1990). How, then, should that radical change be described and understood? Recent literature
tends to emphasize two developments, each characteristic
of modern culture and also mutually dependent. One is the
creation of independent spheres of rationality, beginning as
far back as the fifteenth century, particularly in the area of
politics (the nation-state) and economics (capitalism).
The other is the creation of a social peace on the basis of
tolerance and human rights—an obvious need in Europe
after the wars of religion in the sixteenth and seventeenth
centuries.[1]

The first development set the stage for a way of thinking, characteristic of the Enlightenment, that considers
human reason as a final authority, capable of establishing
its own rules and limits in dealing with the world and with
human life. The point here was not only the decentraliza-
tion of religious authority, but also the abstraction from the
complex wholeness of daily life. Toulmin speaks in this
connection of a decontextualized rationality (1990, 184f.,
200). It was the confidence in this rationality that became
the driving force behind the project of modernity, behind
the growth of an autonomous science and technology, and
behind the organization of society on the basis of progress.
It was a confidence in the possibility of liberating and
humanizing the world. It did not by definition exclude religion, but neither did it need religion to maintain itself.

The second development implied, in fact, the acceptance of religious pluralism and a concept of society as a

system of competition among divergent interests in need of rational management. The destructive effects of the confessional wars could only be overcome by giving up the idea that a culture finds its ultimate unity in a specific religion and by creating, first, the concept of a natural religion common to all human beings and, second, the concept of neutrality of public culture to individual religious preference. Social philosophers refer to this development as the privatization of religion. This terminology suggests a distinction between public life, governed by political and economic rationality, and private life, the only place where religion can still survive.

This brief sketch indicates that the term *secularization* must be used with caution and certainly not in such a way as to suggest that modern culture is characterized by an irreversible trend toward the complete destruction of religion. Obviously, the intriguing tension between modern rationality and religion creates problems for the self-understanding of religion and faith in the modern world. Nevertheless, sweeping statements about these problems are not helpful. The experience of what is generally, but unsatisfactorily, called secularization is at least mixed: there is the promise of liberation and humanization over against all kinds of bondage and oppression, and there is the anxiety of the loss of the certainties of faith, which causes many people to feel homeless in the context of the project of modernity. Therefore, on the level of analysis, the relation between rationality and religion should be treated with great care.

For a theological evaluation of secularization, this implies that there are no easy answers to the question as to how the development of modern culture should be interpreted from the point of view of faith. Neither an unreserved and uncritical baptism of the process nor an equally unreserved and uncritical denunciation of it seems to be helpful. As is well known, both approaches have had—and still have—

their advocates. The first approach claims that secularization is in fact the fulfillment of biblical promises of ridding
the world of religion and of Reformation emphases on
human freedom; it was particularly popular in the 1960s.[2]
The second approach interprets secularization as the
rebellion of a self-styled human autonomy against God and
as a denial of the only possible foundation for human individual and social life. This view has experienced a revival
under the influence of the missionary theologian Lesslie
Newbigin (see Chapter 5). Here, too, on the level of analysis the strengths and weaknesses of both approaches
should be weighed carefully.

Privatization

Although the term *secularization* with all its shortcomings
has gained wide currency, some analysts prefer to speak of
privatization when they describe the radical change in the
relation between religion and modern culture. This draws
our attention not so much to a supposed more or less permanent battle between religious and worldly spheres in
history, but rather to the "pluralization of worlds" as an
important characteristic of a society in which human survival has come to depend on self-sufficient systems of political and economic rationality. In addition, it suggests not so
much the loss or disappearance of religion, but rather the
difficulty of giving religious choices a function of their own
in such a pluralized environment.

The sociologists Berger and Luckmann (Berger and
Luckmann 1966; Berger 1979) argue that individuals in the
modern world are forced to move among a plurality of institutions that no longer form parts of an integrated whole.
Integration can be achieved only on the individual level;
individuals and communities *choose* "plausibility structures" in order to make sense of their world. Because modern society by definition allows for a plurality of such
structures, religion is thereby banished to the private

sphere of life. Briefly stated, the distinction between institutions of *public* rationality and *private* life-worlds is a
basic feature of modernity. Others challenge this distinction by considering the appearance of generalized public
forms of religion, sometimes called civil religion, or by
objecting that the connection between religious conviction
and public participation has never been smooth, and that
even public life is sustained by individual choices.
Nevertheless, it seems to be generally accepted that modern society can be described adequately as a loose arrangement of independently functioning systems, and this
implies the precariousness of at least one of the traditional
public functions of religion—the integration of scattered
life-worlds into one framework.

This approach to the problem of secularization does not
necessarily lead to a call for the restoration of traditional
functions of religion. Its main point is a different one: it
draws attention to the problematic position of individual or
communal life-worlds over against the various systems on
which the life-worlds depend but which undermine their
coherence and integrity by subjecting them to the cold
rationality of politics and economics. This rationality manifests itself in anonymous systems of power (mainly
bureaucratic power) and in the pervasiveness of the effects
of the capitalist economic system, even in daily life. In
other words, the problem of religion is basically connected
to the problem of meaning and identity as such.

Here, too, the outcome seems to be that responsible
management of the problem of secularization takes the
form, not so much of a new religious self-assertion as such,
but rather of a negotiated rearrangement of the relation
between religious conviction and modern rationality. The
most visible example of such a negotiated rearrangement
is, of course, fundamentalism in its various forms. As we
will have occasion to point out in this book, fundamentalism should not be understood as a rebellion of religion

against modernity, but rather as an effort to conquer modern rationality and to place it at the service of a particular, idealized religious tradition. It rather drastically solves the problem of the pluralism of systems and of privatization.

There are, undoubtedly, other ways of solving the problem. It seems safe to say that, whatever way is chosen, it will necessarily involve a basic rethinking of the role of faith among and vis-à-vis the various public rational systems that constitute the fabric of modern culture.

Functional Rationality

An important element in the analysis of secularization is the insight that modern rationality has come to dominate social and cultural life in a special way, generally designated as functional or instrumental. Functional rationality may be described as a permanent critical reflection that tests actions and ideas in comparison with their intentions and effects. It is geared toward the efficient and effective realization of goals and tends to suppress critical discussion about the choice of those goals. Functional rationality is the driving force of the various systems, specifically the political and the economic systems; it is the immanent dynamic by which these systems keep themselves going. It is the instrument of the technological management of human life.

Functional rationality is the feature of modern culture that has been the target of several critics of the so-called Enlightenment project. In their 1944 classic essay; *Dialektik der Aufklaerung (The Dialectics of the Enlightenment)*, Max Horkheimer and Theodor Adorno analyzed the rise of functional rationality as the tragedy of bourgeois civilization—tragedy, because this form of rationality inevitably leads to the dominion of irrationality in the form of new myths. The will to rationalize, to manage, and to control results in new forms of slavery because it narrows the potential of human rationality and as such undermines the human capacity for constructive communication.

Jürgen Habermas is one of the contemporary social philosophers who have elaborated on this approach. He has tried to overcome its tragic aspects by developing a theory of rational communication that accounts for both the negative effects and the creative possibilities of the Enlightenment project. Yet he, too, states clearly that the cognitive-instrumental one-sidedness of the modern concept of rationality reflects the objective bias of the capitalist organization of life (Habermas 1985; generally: 1981). Along this line Habermas develops his view of the antagonism between systems and "life-world." He calls this antagonism "colonization." Life-world is the as yet undifferentiated cohesion of human communication that, in the growing complexity of modern society, is gradually organized through the differentiation and institutionalization of systems. This process, however, reaches its limit when the coherence of the life-world itself begins to be threatened. That is colonization.

These and similar views reflect the widespread experience that fundamental layers of human life, although dependent for their survival precisely on the effectiveness and efficiency of the various systems, are under heavy pressure. In its most personal dimensions, human life in modern culture has become vulnerable to politicizing and economizing, to becoming a mere plaything of impersonal processes.

In a discussion about changes in the relation between religion and rationality, a focus on functional rationality, in connection with the previously discussed item of privatization, is of paramount importance. The more thoughtful analysts of the process of secularization, rather than proclaiming the gradual disappearance of religion, observe that religion changes its behavior under the pressure of functional rationality. It tends more and more to leave the

various autonomous systems of rationality to function, as it
were, by themselves: sometimes it seeks public and institutional expression under the conditions of functional
rationality in order to survive; often it is on the retreat in
order to reassess and rearrange its own business.

The analysis of functional rationality summarized
above, however, suggests that a mere retreat into the private sphere would amount to a surrender to something like
the death of the human being. In other words, the challenge to rethink the place and function of religion in the
changed context of modern culture is important for culture
itself. This is not to say that only religion can save culture.
Habermas, for one, works out his solutions by explicitly
excluding the role of religion. But at least for those who
take the claims of much traditional religion seriously,
analyses like the one by Habermas can offer new insights
as to the direction that the rearrangement of the relation
between religion and rationality ought to take.

Secularization Revisited

Our sketch so far has indicated that it is premature to say
that our culture has become or is becoming secular, worldly, in the sense that religion is on its way out. It is certainly not premature to say, however, that the project of
modernity has upset and is upsetting traditional social
structures to such an extent that those interested in religion are forced to rethink its place and function in a fundamental way. Now that the project of modernity as such
has come under fire from various sides in what is often
called postmodern approaches, it is perhaps possible to
embark on this adventure in a way that avoids the two pitfalls already mentioned: baptizing or denouncing the
process as such. In a sense, these pitfalls are part of the
project of modernity; in any case, they bear its marks.

The effort to rethink the relation between religion and
rationality should avoid sharp dichotomies and include at

least some of the ambivalence produced by the development of modern culture as such. On the one hand, the loose arrangement of rational systems, notably the systems of the national state and the capitalist economy, have produced and still are producing a certain amount of emancipation, humanization, and stability. On the other hand, the functional rationality that increasingly characterizes these systems threatens the survival of the basic values of human life. Oppression and violence, widely experienced in today's world, can to a large extent be directly related to this aspect of modernity. How can religion account for this ambivalence and at the same time do justice to its traditional claim of maintaining some wholeness and perspective in human life?

Concentrating the treatment of secularization on the relation of religion and rationality avoids yet another blind alley in the discussion: the restriction of the phenomenon of secularization to modern Europe and the belief that modern America is different in the sense that in that culture the vitality of religion has not been impaired. If one would take the term *secularization* literally, as referring to something like a territorial battle between worldliness and religion, then to a certain extent the distinction might hold. The history of modern Europe has indeed been characterized by much more antagonism between religion and public life than that of the United States, where examples of fruitful covenants between Enlightenment, religion, and public life abound—in spite of the separation of church and state. However, against the background of the analysis of modern society as a loose arrangement of systems and the lostness of religion in that context, both cultures turn out to be very similar. On the surface, because of the different histories, the adjustment of religion to modern culture may be more successful in America than in Europe; the basic problems are nevertheless quite comparable.

In summary, we must distinguish two levels in both the experience and the concept of secularization. The first level is the emancipation of modern rationality from religion in a general way; life can be organized without reference to religion. This emancipation can lead to religious enthusiasm, but also to feelings of lostness and uncertainty. The second level is the narrowing of modern rationality, showing its problematic nature as an instrument for the technological management of life, with all its accompanying characteristics of domination, exclusion, and oppression. Our real problem lies on the second level. Therefore, when a reassessment of the relation between religion and rationality is called for, the point is not the defense of religion over against an increase of worldliness, but rather an inquiry into the nature of true worldliness and true rationality and into the possible function of religion against that background.

Notes

1. This is the central point in Pannenberg's essay (1989).

2. One example out of many: Cox 1965.

2

Religion, Rationality, and Faith

After our brief and admittedly incomplete review of terms and theories in relation to secularization in the first chapter, the aim of this second chapter is twofold: to look more closely at the changed relation between religion and rationality and to consider the necessity of defining faith as not identical with either religion or rationality. Both exercises are necessary for the understanding of the problem of secularization and for the further qualification of its definition.

Religion

Up to this point, our argument has left the term *religion* largely undefined, which is of course quite unsatisfactory. In sociological literature about the problem of secularization, the term *religion* is generally used to cover both the general human search for transcendent points of reference and the institutions that channel and regulate this search. On a more philosophical level, there is an obvious need for further refinement and differentiation. If one wants to understand and interpret religious plurality, that is, the diversity of designs that are applied to what seems to be a general human quest, one is driven in the direction of isolating something like "basic experiences" or "fundamental questions," and to consider those separately from their

11

various interpretations and institutionalizations (Tracy 1987, chap. 5; Vroom 1989: chap. 9). "Isolating" may not be the correct term, for we know that experience and interpretation provoke and determine each other. Yet there is a difference—between the mobility and pluriformity of religious activity on the most basic level and the relative unity and cohesiveness of a religious worldview or institution—that must be taken into consideration. Mobility and cohesiveness may not be present or even conceivable apart from each other, but they do represent two aspects that live in a dynamic tension. The difference between the two aspects takes on special significance in the perspective of our analysis of secularization. As we will see, it is a difference in relation to rationality.

Religion in its most basic sense, then, refers to the human preoccupation with finitude, failure, suffering, the encounter of good and evil, the experience of love and anxiety. Religion is the constant struggle with radical contingency. The struggle expresses itself primarily in a loose variety of activities and ideas that might be characterized as symbolic-ritual. This variety then produces the basic material for larger and more sophisticated systems of meaning, but underneath this streamlining and sophistication it continues a life of its own, as is documented by the history of all great faiths. The faiths incorporate, interpret, and unite religious activities in larger cognitive frameworks that intend to express and sustain the basic religious intuition that there is an ultimate wholeness and coherence in the world and in human life. Yet in doing this, they never fully reconcile or transcend the diversity. In other words, the tension between "basic religion" and "streamlining faith" is permanent. The great religions or faiths—Islam, Christianity, Buddhism, Judaism, and Hinduism—are in fact complicated systems in which this permanent tension is shaped in particular ways.

Anthropologists teach us that basic religion has been

the driving force behind human rationality. Rationality, generally speaking, is the human capacity to organize and understand, to apply logical connections to a seemingly chaotic world, to establish communication according to accepted rules, and to cultivate things according to preconceived plans. This rationality has its origin in the religious desire to conceive of meaning and coherence and to master and manipulate the more elusive aspects of life. Priest and scholar derive from the same basic figure. In this way it becomes understandable that religion and rationality have maintained a relationship of kinship and hostility throughout the history of civilization. The perennial secularizing aspects of human rationality have always threatened religion to some extent; but wherever the balance was kept or restored, it was to the benefit of both.

It is precisely this balance that seems to be breaking down in modern culture. Modern rationality, in its tendency to decontextualize and to elevate itself above the chaotic complexity of the "life-worlds," has come to distrust religion and its claims to coherence and wholeness. There is no peaceful coexistence, no creative tension; the systems that thrive on rationality almost by definition try to reduce religion to a harmless phenomenon.

This does not mean that religion has disappeared or is disappearing. Rather, it has become homeless; its variety of expressions no longer connects to culture in a self-evident and generally accepted way.

Faith

The preceding section argues the legitimacy of differentiating between "the mobility and pluriformity of religious activity on the most basic level and the relative unity and cohesiveness of a religious worldview or institution," and it draws attention to a permanent tension between basic religion and structuring systems of meaning. This differentiation, of course, confounds the definition of religion, because the latter term is commonly used for both aspects. Yet this is precisely the point at which it becomes helpful, at least according to the argument presented here, to specify the meaning of the term *faith* as distinct from *religion*.

We define faith as the structuring of religious activities by way of a tradition, a community, a story, a truth, or a revelation. The emphasis falls on streamlining and organizing and on larger frameworks of meaning. In more complex societies, such frameworks tend to assume social, cultural, even political significance and to compete with the rational systems that are developed in those societies. Faith refers to a system in which all aspects of reality—the ends of the earth and the end of time—are drawn together into one perspective, a perspective to which believers respond with trust and loyalty, and in which they find their spiritual home.

The point of the distinction is that speaking about religion or faith makes a difference with regard to rationality. There is a different relation. Against the background of the original balance and tension between religion and rationality, faith tends to be on both sides at the same time. Structuring and integrating religion into larger frameworks is an aspect of the rational organization of life, and it easily allies itself with the more secular aspects of rationalization. Faith and rationality have a certain affinity: both are preoccupied with the grand stories (Lyotard), the overarching interpretations of reality. Faith and rationality stimulate each other in a kind of competition and at times condemn each other. Sometimes—particularly in the context of modern culture—they share a certain suspicion with regard to religion. In general, faith functions as a bridge, an intermediate form, between religion and rationality. As long as the bridge is strong, it contributes to the well-being of the balance between religion and rationality, to the benefit of both. However, the alliance with the more secular aspects of rationalization can also become a movement away from the "ways of life" of religion, and it can even take the form of a manipulation of those ways.

It might be objected, at this point, that it is practically impossible to conceive of religion apart from some form of faith, and that this makes the distinction artificial. The objection is pertinent to the extent that the distinction at first sight does not correspond to social facts. Neither can it be denied, even if the distinction is granted some validity, that it is never clear-cut: there are only gradual transitions between more basic and more sophisticated forms of religion. Why, then, is it necessary to introduce and maintain the distinction?

The answer is that it is precisely modern (functional) rationality that drives a wedge between the two aspects or functions of the religious life under discussion. The two have always stayed together very closely; it is modern rationality that provokes and reveals the distinction between the organizing story aspect of the religious life and the more basic religious aspect. Modern rationality retains its affinity with the former and begins to mistrust and alienate the latter. The more developed and sophisticated forms of religion participate in typical products of modern rationality such as scientific explanation and institutional management, whereas the more basic forms of religion are made homeless *by precisely these products.* If one wants to do justice to this observation and to pursue the analysis of secularization along this line, some distinction is inevitable and might yet prove fruitful.

The distinction between faith and religion that is attempted here does not intend to come anywhere near the more normative theological distinctions, as for instance the one employed by Karl Barth (1936, ¶17). Barth's point is that *faith* is the freedom, granted by grace, to hear the word of God, and *religion* is the perennial human tendency to subject this word to the conditions of human thinking and human desire. This distinction can

have an important function within the confines of the
Christian faith-system: it can contribute to a better understanding of the relation between God and the human being
as it is conceived in this system. But it cannot and does not
clarify the relation of religion (generally speaking) and
modern rationality.

The distinction suggested in this essay is closer to the
one between faith and "cumulative tradition" proposed by
Wilfred Cantwell Smith (1964; 1981). (We would, obviously, replace "faith" by "religion" and "cumulative tradition"
by "faith.") However, there is a difference of emphasis here
too. Smith's distinction intends to criticize the tendency to
absolutize certain cumulative traditions in a dogmatic way
and, behind that, the tendency to hypostasize religious systems. With his overemphasis on a universal human process
of religious learning ("faith," in his terms) he forfeits the
possibility to differentiate within this process of learning
between several constitutive elements. And this is precisely what the distinction proposed here intends to do.

We return to the designation of faith as a bridge
between religion and rationality. If secularization can
rightly be interpreted as a serious disturbance in the balance between religion and rationality, it can also be said
that the disturbance has serious consequences for the
function of the bridge. The bridge can no longer perform
its task adequately. In other words, it loses its public significance. That is precisely what we see happening in the
process of secularization.

There may be yet another side to this. As already indicated, faith has always been in alliance with rationality.
This has remained so, even during the development of
modern culture. Perhaps we have to conclude that this
alliance has become too strong. Perhaps faith has become
contaminated by the negative features of modern functional rationality. It could be that because of this, faith has
become less trustworthy from the point of view of religion.

If this suggestion is valid, then the crisis of faith, which is an essential aspect of what is generally called secularization, cannot be blamed on the development of modern rationality only. *It is a problem of balance between religion, rationality, and faith, and as such it has been a problem of Western culture all along.*

A Closer Profile

Because the distinction between religion and faith appears to be helpful in the analysis of the relation between religion and rationality in the context of modern culture, we might also consider its usefulness for the understanding of the basic human activity of interpreting the world and attributing meaning to it. The distinction may have been provoked and revealed by modern rationality; but once we have it, we can use it in hindsight and look upon the three elements—religion, rationality, and faith—as the permanent instruments of the search for and construction of meaning. In the course of history, the elements may have been valued and emphasized in different ways; they may have formed configurations widely divergent among themselves. But if it makes sense to establish their continuous presence, this might enable us to place the experience of secularization more clearly in historical perspective.

The most intriguing transitions in the history of human thought have been the transition from symbolic-ritual meaning to narrative-mythical interpretation, and subsequently the one from myth to a more abstract rationality. Each transition exposes the previous phase as being less adequate, further away from truth finding, and yet traces of each phase remain recognizably present. Modern Enlightenment-rationality has tended to regard the whole history of thought as a pilgrimage of humankind toward higher forms of dealing with reality, and itself as the goal of that pilgrimage. Postmodern criticism is more inclined to vindicate the permanent significance of all phases.

Myth and narrative are obviously a first attempt at rationalization in the sense of bringing some order and coherence to the interpretation of reality. In the history of
ancient Greece we observe that this attempt had a secularizing effect on less differentiated religious worldviews, and
it was secularized in turn by the subsequent development
of the more abstract rationality of the philosophers. In this
perspective, religion, faith, and rationality present themselves as three successive layers in a historical process, as
human instruments that gradually unfold and become distinct, after having been active in a kind of unproblematic
symbiosis. They remain active as the struggle with radical
contingency, as narrative structuring, and as argumenta-
tive ordering, respectively. Together the instruments form
configurations, with the aid of which human beings interpret their worlds, both at the individual or communal level
or at the level of cultural and religious systems. In the different configurations the three elements can be emphasized and balanced in many different ways. Even in the
context of modern culture this process continues. Religion
needs faith and rationality in order to keep it from producing impetuous and chaotic movements. Rationality needs
religion and faith in order to keep it from reducing human
life to impersonal calculation. Faith needs religion and
rationality if it is to serve complete humanization.

As soon as we establish the existence of configurations
of religion, rationality, and faith as instruments of meaning, we have to remind ourselves that there has also
always been a great variety of such configurations within
the confines of particular cultural and religious systems.
The diversity of configurations on all levels of human life
implies permanent struggle and conflict. To some extent
questions of truth have always been questions of power, of
dominance of certain configurations over others. That is
true for individual lives: personal configurations of meaning are involved in processes of adjustment, conflict,

search for stability and continuity, and they are constantly challenged by particular developments on other levels of the articulation of meaning. It is also true for communities and cultures. In the permanent search and struggle for meaning there is the possibility that for a certain period of time a specific configuration promises stability and as such gains influence and power. In this sense one can speak of configurations of meaning that dominate a particular culture or a particular period. Yet even then, the variety of configurations and the permanence of the struggle for truth and meaning among individuals and communities, behind an apparently uniform facade, remains a strong dynamic for change.

Against this background, the problem of secularization of the relation between religion and rationality in the context of modern culture appears to be a fundamental disturbance in the ongoing production of meaning. The disturbance is created by the dominance of a more decisively emancipated rationality, which, with its distrust of religion and myth, tends to upset the precarious balance of the three elements.

Secularization Revisited

The remark that the balance of the three elements has been a problem of Western culture all along still awaits some clarification. How can it be squared with the suggestion that the three elements are characteristic of human culture as such, and that they are universal instruments of the search for meaning?

Perhaps the answer is that the history of Western culture has been characterized by three heritages that are basically incompatible. One is the Jewish-Christian tradition of an eschatological spirituality, which views human life in the perspective of judgment and promise; another one is the Greek-Roman way of questioning and searching for meaning and coherence; and finally there is the heritage of Gnostic religiosity, which continues to be relevant.

The various syntheses formed by these different heritages have produced impressive forms of culture: that is true for the Hellenistic, the medieval, and the modern-bourgeois synthesis. Yet they have also produced conflicts, revolutions, and renewals—Renaissance, Reformation, and Enlightenment are the most important ones. Those conflicts, revolutions, and renewals always implied an upsetting and a fundamental rearrangement of the three elements.

On the threshold of the modern-bourgeois synthesis, the relations between religion, rationality, and faith were very good; one only needs to think of the enthusiastic speculations and religious prophecies resulting from the French revolution; of rationality as new religion; of the many attempts to harmonize traditional faith with the promises of modern rationality. There were conflicts, such as the one between Bible-criticism and fundamentalism, and there were oppositional religious subcultures in revival movements and sects. In hindsight, these can be regarded as early signals of a more basic tension between religion and modern rationality. By and large, however, modern Christianity was characterized by a positive relation between faith and rationality, and this relation was able for a long time to overshadow the emerging tensions.

The problem of secularization appears in the framework of the modern-bourgeois synthesis. Still, it would be short-sighted to attribute its rise solely to the Enlightenment, as if this were an external hostile power entering Western history with the intention of destroying traditional faith and religion. As has been pointed out, the situation is considerably more complex. The Enlightenment is also a symptom of a problem that has been there all along. It is perhaps more adequate to say that the tensions inherent in the modern synthesis, specifically those elicited by the development of functional rationality, reveal the difficulty of achieving an adequate balance of religion, rationality, and faith in a fundamental and decisive way.

At one level, it might be sufficient to say that the new situation simply presents the challenge for another rearrangement of the three elements. In several communities and subcultures, creative attempts can indeed be found to work with new configurations in which religion and rationality are related in different ways. At the same time, however, it must be underlined that it is modern rationality that has revealed the problem of the balance in a fundamental way and that has introduced a basic ambivalence in all attempts to deal with it. Modern rationality almost by definition qualifies both religion and faith as highly problematic approaches to reality. And precisely in this way it confirms its own problematic status. In other words, the ambivalence is there to stay.

3

The Global Perspective

The previous chapters approached the problem of secularization as a problem of modern Western culture, and rightly so. Although tensions between religion and rationality (including secularization in a general sense) can be found at all times and all places, the specific problem we have examined is characteristic for the West. For an adequate analysis of secularization, however, this observation is not sufficient, especially if the analysis is supposed to lead toward further reflection on mission. We will have to take account of the fact that the Western problem has become a global problem. This third chapter intends to do just that. It raises the question: in what sense can and must secularization be understood as a global problem, and how does it influence our involvement in intercultural communication?

Asymmetry

It has been argued that the modernization that took place in the context of Western culture led to globalization on the strength of its own dynamics. The two basic ingredients of modernization—the nation-state and the capitalist economic system—could afford to ignore the territorial limits of the traditional organization of society; in other words, they had the logic of expansion built into them. The shift to functional priorities in politics and economics by itself relativized all ordering of a more hierarchical nature. Functional rationality *by its own nature* moves toward further goals, wider communication, more markets.

Insofar as this argument suggests that the export of the benefits of Western culture to other parts of the world was a smooth and self-evident affair, it is, of course, quite incomplete. To be sure, it is good to keep in mind that there is a certain logic to Western expansion, and that this logic lies precisely in the changing function of rationality that we have discussed. But it cannot be ignored that this logic manifested itself in the form of an often violent colonialism and imperialism. The violence was (and is) not only political, military, and racial, but also, in a deeper sense, cultural. What that means can perhaps be best expressed with the aid of the configuration model developed in the preceding chapter. The implication of Western expansion is that the typically Western disturbance of the balance between religion, rationality, and faith establishes itself on a global scale and as such threatens to undermine the various balances present in non-Western cultures.

This is not the same thing as saying that the process of secularization is conquering the world in an inescapable and unambiguous movement. That is not the case. What is the case is that Western modernity has saddled the world with a problem that might mean different things to different cultures, but that can nowhere be simply suppressed or ignored. The problem begins with the availability and the attractiveness of the various functional rationalities of the expanding systems, and it moves toward the necessity for non-Western societies to avail themselves of those rationalities in order to survive. All this takes place in the context of cultures that are prepared, even less than Western culture, for the unsettling effects of modernity. Whatever balances there are between religion and rationality and faith in non-Western cultures have all been challenged to readjustment or reassertion. Solutions vary widely, but the problem is the same.

Against this background it is not difficult to understand the emergence of movements that, beyond decolonization and liberation, proclaim the rejection of all modern Western influence. More precisely, they reject Westernization and welcome modernization. Such a formula presupposes that it is possible to have the one without the other. This of course is open to discussion. But it indicates the deep longing to be delivered from the pressure of the Western incompatibility of religion and rationality.

It is tempting at this point to elaborate on fundamentalism as a possible example of such a movement. In the first chapter it was suggested that fundamentalism should not be understood as a simple rebellion of religion against modernity, but rather as an effort to conquer modern rationality and to place it at the service of a particular, idealized religious tradition. In other words, it seeks an alternative connection of faith and rationality and to that extent presupposes the globalization of modernity. It balances between self-assertion and emulation. It uses the same playing cards as secularization does, but it shuffles them differently.

There is still another aspect of secularization in global perspective that is relevant in the context of the present discussion. Closely related to the balance-disturbing effects of the logic of expansion is a certain blindness in modern Western culture to non-Western configurations and a persistent inability to take those seriously. This built-in tendency to cultural, ethnic, and racial exclusion is one of the paradoxes of modernity. The project of modernity prides itself on its universality and yet ignores and denies "the other"—that which does not adapt itself to modern standards and cannot be accommodated in modern frameworks. The paradox is characteristic of a cul-

ture that allows itself to be managed by "functional rationality." This rationality is universal by nature; it globalizes
automatically, but rejects what it regards as inferior rationalities. In this way the paradox extends itself. Even in its
worldwide expansion, modern culture is in the process of
alienating itself from the rest of the world.

This paradox of intolerance has been exposed and crit-
icized not only from the outside, from the side of the
excluded (such as blacks), but also from within, by various
movements and subcultures (such as women). These have
tried and are trying to advocate alternative configurations
of religion, rationality, and faith. By implication, they are
searching for alternative ways of globalization—ways that
might produce a better balance between rational communication and cultural pluralism.

The problem of secularization in global perspective is
precisely that this balance is missing. There is an obvious
asymmetry between Western and non-Western cultures.
No analysis of globalization and intercultural communication can afford to pass this over.

Globalization

It has been suggested that globalization by itself raises a
new religious question (Robertson 1985, 347–58; 1990,
63–77). The point of this suggestion is that the expansion
of the systems of modern society into global networks creates a new context of experience that can be characterized
as eschatologically open. On the one hand, the new context
of global communication exposes the arbitrariness of all
given religious traditions; on the other hand, it opens a discussion on the nature and destiny of *humankind.*
Analogously, on the one hand, the development of global
networks exposes people's individuality as it relativizes
their roots; on the other hand, it opens up more possibilities
for community building. The discussion on human-kind will
inevitably be shaped by the interaction of concepts and

images that are entertained by the various cultural and religious communities, but in the process these communities will be confronted with essentially new questions.

In connection with this approach, a recent book by Peter Beyer (1993) takes up the question as to how religion can exercise public influence in a global society. Beyer's thesis is that religion is subject to privatization to the extent it is considered as a functional subsystem in modern society, but that it can be influential as a "socio-cultural particularism." This term refers to the way in which specific traditions and values work in society—pervasively, and in the background, as a cultural resource for various systems, but without themselves becoming part of the "world of systems." Beyer argues that religiously based social movements, focusing for instance on peace and ecology, are the obvious channels for the public influence of religion in global society. They have their source in the lifeworlds that have not been completely captivated and colonized by the world of systems.

We may have a useful way here of speaking about the global perspective of the problem of secularization. Using our own terminology we may try it out as follows.

The problem of the disturbed balance between religion and rationality becomes quite complex when considered on a global scale, that is, in the context of a pluriform and never-ending battle of configurations. Speaking positively, the pluriformity of the battle means that there is a large variety of religious sources to draw on, and all these sources are challenged *to develop faith-concepts in relation to the unity of humankind.* To put it differently, the alienating effects of the global networks of functional rationality call for interreligious alliances on a global scale, particularly alliances between forms of religion that survive in modern Western culture and forms of religion that have different cultural histories and may be part of stronger balanced configurations. The aim of the alliances cannot be the neutralization of functional rationality, for this rationality has become the basic instrument for the survival of the human race; but the aim can be its containment, that is, the surveillance of its proper confines. The alliances cannot take away the ambivalence in all matters of religion and faith, which is an ineradicable effect of modernity, but they can become countermovements against it. On this basis, the new discussions about the nature and destiny of humankind might become new bridges of faith that challenge all particular faith-traditions and equip them for new roles and new configurations.

The thesis that modernization and secularization automatically entail globalization can also be turned around. Globalization itself has a secularizing effect, in the sense that new networks of reflection about human life come into being that encompass, precede, challenge, and influence all institutionalized religion and faith. As long as this is not taken seriously, intercultural communication will not be successful, and particular faith-traditions will not be able to handle their crises. Perhaps it can be said that the secularizing effect of globalization counteracts the negative effects of the globalization of secularization, as it makes intercultural and interreligious alliances possible.

Intercultural Communication

Intercultural communication is a basic fact of human history. Ontologically, if not historically, it precedes the formation of cultures as separate units. Cultures are temporary fixations in a continuing process of communication; and even here the term *fixation* is wrong, for cultures themselves can be described as dynamic processes, always in some relation with each other. If this intuition is at all valid, we may continue to state that secularization in global perspective amounts to the reactivation of this intercultural communication under special conditions—the conditions of the expansion of modernity.

What is complicating here is the fact that the very definition of the word *culture* took place under the conditions
of modernity. To call a certain system of beliefs, habits, and
styles a culture was a function of awakening modern rationality; it was the expression of the self-understanding of
bourgeois society. To study these cultures and to arrange
them in some sort of over-arching system in relation to the
culture doing the studying (modern Western science)
implied almost by definition a biased way of studying and
the development of stereotypes. In fact, the Western design
of a "history of cultures" legitimized the incorporation of
the non-Western world into the modern systems of political and economic rationality. Forms of construction of
meaning that were discovered in other cultures—symbolic-ritual forms and narrative-mythical forms—were distin-
guished from Western rationality, not only historically, but
also logically, and they were, by implication, considered
inferior.

The Dutch philosopher of culture, Ton Lemaire, con-
structs a philosophical approach to intercultural communication on the basis of this fundamental complication
(Lemaire 1976). His thesis is that the history of cultural
anthropology as a science reflects the problem of modernity and witnesses to the crisis in which modern Western culture finds itself. Particularly intriguing is his treatment of
the Western philosophical movements that react against
the view that Western rationality is the climax of human
history. By their reaction they destroy historical consciousness: existentialism, structuralism, and various
forms of relativism. According to Lemaire, cultural relativism emerged as a reaction against the philosophical and
scientific legitimation of colonialism. It did not, however,
offer a tenable alternative. It amounted to "serial and
inevitable ethnocentrism" and did not deal constructively
with cultural interaction. It was no more than the "unhap-
py consciousness of colonialism," although it did take one

step in the direction of a non-European–centered view of history. More important steps were taken by those philosophical movements that made alienation a central theme and began to criticize the whole modern Western project from within. Freud and Nietzsche, the "masters of suspicion," and the various postmodern schools that have developed in their wake are of particular importance here. Can modern rationality be called progress? Was it perhaps a mistake to project alienation one-sidedly on non-Western cultures?

Lemaire's searching questions confirm our insight that the cultural plurality of our world is not a simple or innocent plurality; it can be dealt with adequately only if it is placed in the inescapable context of the problem of Western rationality. This is not a context that places Western culture outside of the problem, in an invulnerable position. On the contrary, the global perspective of secularization raises major issues for all cultures, including the modern West. In this global perspective the problem of secularization becomes the problem of the conditions for a tenable unity of humankind.

Secularization Revisited

The expansion of modernity is an obvious and inescapable framework for unity; what we have today in terms of global cohesiveness and intercultural communication has been realized by its instruments. At the same time, the expansion of modernity has created, and still creates, major problems precisely for that cohesiveness and communication. It does not foster a tenable balance of unity and plurality; it does not preclude violence; it increasingly captivates and colonizes life-worlds. It may seem a gross exaggeration, at the conclusion of this chapter, to subsume all this under the problem of secularization (we have really moved a great distance from the original meaning of the term!). Nevertheless, as has been the consistent argument throughout the three chapters, if we focus on the problem behind the more ephemeral experiences of secularization—that is, the disturbed relation between religion and rationality—a whole chain of problems offers itself for clarification in that perspective, and it is inevitable that we end up speaking about the unity of humankind.

Religious plurality is marginalized, made insignificant and arbitrary by the global systems of rationality; and yet it is a major source for a unity that is not carried through at the expense of a plurality that thrives on the vitality of life-worlds. If *faiths* have a role to play in the future, it is the role of building new bridges between living religious plurality on the one hand and the dominant systems of rationality on the other. Secularization reactivates intercultural communication; this intercultural communication must be turned against its destructive tendencies.

Unity of humankind requires the art of combining two apparently contradictory projects. One is bringing together people, nations, and races in an effective and efficient system of communication that produces and promotes justice. The other is taking seriously people, nations, and races in their genuine particularity, their distinctiveness. Human history so far has been able only to realize one project at the expense of the other, which is one way of explaining the inevitability of violence. The art of combining the two contradictory ideas (bringing people together while taking seriously their distinctiveness) requires, at the philosophical and theological level, a serious confrontation with the problem of secularization, which should be designated more precisely as the problem of religion, rationality, and faith.

4

Mission: Crisis and Kairos

The modern missionary movement, which began to flour-
ish in the eighteenth century, can be looked at in two ways.
On the one hand, as a project of spreading the Christian
faith from a Western home base, it clearly demonstrates
the alliance of faith and modern rationality and, in that
respect, participates in the export of the Western problem
as analyzed in the preceding chapters. On the other hand,
at least implicitly, it has prepared the way for genuine
encounter and dialogue, for the discovery of the particu-
larities of non-Western configurations of religion, rationality,
and faith, and for a fundamental reconsideration of the
place of Christian faith in an essentially pluralistic world.
Now that the negative effects of the alliance between faith
and modern rationality are being exposed in various ways,
and the question of the possibility of a sensible intercultural communication is raised anew, it is of paramount
importance to capitalize on this latter aspect and not to get
stuck in facile judgments with regard to the former.

This fourth chapter intends to sketch the learning
process that is involved and that gradually got underway in
the course of the twentieth century. It deals with the significance of some basic experiences of the missionary
movement, such as de-territorialization, pluralization, and

globalization; it does this against the background of the
preceding analysis of secularization in order to specify
the challenges faced in any contemporary discussion on
mission.

Mission Domesticated

In the ecumenical movement that began to take shape after
the First World War, mission was a dominant concern. The
first world conferences on mission, particularly the ones in
Jerusalem (1928) and Tambaram (1938), reflect the effort
to safeguard and develop the missionary movement on the
basis of a deepened analysis of various world problems. It
is important to note that secularization begins to play an
important role in this analysis. Secularization was designated as a worldwide civilization, advocating the possibility of life without God or religion, and in that respect as the
major rival of Christian mission. This analysis led to a concept of Christianity as a model for a global society, called to
permanent witness in order to save the world from secularization, pagan ideologies, and misleading religions. For
this witness both old and young churches would have to
create a living network of hope. It was this concept that
came to dominate ecumenical institutions, including the
International Missionary Council. It led the explosive variety of the earlier missionary movements into the channels
of a global organization of churches, which were seen as
the preeminent agencies for mission. It brought "mission"
and "church" close together. It implied that religions were
mainly regarded as rivals to be brought under the claim of
Christ, just like secular civilization. It stimulated the para-
digmatic option for what Konrad Raiser (1991) calls "chris-
tocentric universalism," which became the integrating
vision of the ecumenical movement for decades to come.

In hindsight, two things can be observed about this ecumenical paradigm. First, although secularization is rightly
recognized as a global problem that should lead to a

rethinking of mission, the analysis of the problem is clearly deficient. The significance of the alliance of dominant forms of Christian faith and theology with modern rationality is as yet unrecognized and underestimated. In fact, by the designation of secularization as a rival civilization, this alliance is confirmed and strengthened. Theoretically, it would have been possible to construct the ecumenical movement as a network of communication on the basis of a universal human religious search. That would have been a way to incorporate the essential experience of pluralism in the missionary movement. But the missionary movement was, in a sense, taken over by the rationality of global institutional management. In choosing this direction, the resulting ecumenical movement could not dissociate itself sufficiently from the project of modernity and from its characteristic suspicion of religion. Second, the ecumenical paradigm brought the missionary movement into a more mature phase, in the sense that its spirituality of conquest was gradually replaced by an awareness of the global systems with which it had to come to terms. This happened, however, at the expense of its capacity for spontaneous dialogue and its capacity for seeking points of contact on the level of religion. Meanwhile, the more evangelical wing of the missionary movement remained suspicious of this whole ecumenical development and thus retained some of the original strength of pre-ecumenical missions; but it paid the price of remaining largely outside of the ecumenical learning process.

Mission, then, was domesticated by an ecumenical paradigm that was characterized by the rediscovery of the church as the essential unit of witness and by a concept of global salvation history with the reigning Christ at its center. The concept of *missio Dei* served to express the coherence of these elements, and a continuing discussion on the relation between mission and unity became necessary. Against the background of serious challenges to

the missionary movement (Second World War, decolonization, the "loss" of China) the whole paradigm became a
powerful tool to create a broad and strong ecumenical
movement. At the same time, it can be observed in hindsight
that the vagueness and pliability of the *missio Dei* concept,
as well as the unsolvability of the mission-unity question,
signaled the incompleteness of the learning process.

New Openings

The picture began to change when two things began to
claim special attention in the framework of the institutionalized ecumenical movement: the issue of development
and world poverty, and the challenge of interreligious dialogue. Both, of course, have their natural place in the missionary movement; but their separate structuring within
the World Council of Churches highlighted important tensions in the original concept of mission and thus served as
a new stimulus for the learning process. In this separate
structuring it became clear that the two terms *poverty* and
dialogue reflect major concerns of non-Western Christians
and therefore just might herald an alternative way of looking
at the problem of mission in the context of global systems.

What is new here, although certainly not universally
recognized, is the focus on the contextual struggle for survival and on the basic human religious search as two constitutive elements for the definition of Christian faith in
global perspective. This focus challenges the major presuppositions of the missionary and ecumenical movements as
these had developed under the protection of the project of
modernity. It opens the possibility of speaking about long-
familiar concepts such as salvation, conversion, and witness in new ways.

Implied above all is a new and deeper level of confrontation with the problem of secularization. This will
require some explanation, because the term *secularization*
seldom figures in the discussions on poverty and dialogue.

The argument in the preceding section was that the designation of secularization as a rival civilization in fact implied a confirmation of the alliance of faith and modern rationality and thus an acceptance of the terms of modernity. (This, by the way, is illustrated by the positive use of secularization in the study project "Missionary Structures of the Congregation" of the 1960s.) What increasingly happened as the voice of the Third World became stronger in ecumenical discussions around 1970 was that the whole use of Western rationality was placed under criticism. In other words, the worldwide civilization is still a strong rival of Christian missions, but it is no longer its God-less or antireligious character that is most threatening, but rather its *Western* character and the ambivalence that is created by the alliance of missions with Western rationality and its suspicion of religion. The world mission conference of Bangkok (1972) was a significant turning point. From then on, ecumenical discussions from the point of view of the Third World increasingly expose the captivity of the classical ecumenical movement to the project of modernity. From this, the new emphasis on *poverty* and *dialogue* takes on special significance.

We might illustrate this significance in the following way. One of the most influential contributions of the modern missionary movement to the self-consciousness of Christianity—although not yet generally acknowledged, let alone appropriated—is the de-territorialization of Christian faith; in other words, the denial of the essential nature of any link between a certain faith and a certain territory. This in itself, of course, is a modern view, firmly established in Western culture after the confessional wars. But in the missionary movement it meant that conquest for Christ does not necessarily imply territorial conquest, and—just as important—it does not necessarily imply a reproduction of any particular Christ-culture establishment. Missionaries have not always lived up to this insight;

nevertheless, the movement as such became a living proof of it. This insight meant the acceptance of pluralism as a basic feature, not only of the world as such, but also of world-Christianity. Global conquest implied contextual variety.

As we have seen, the first major step in the ecumenical learning process led to a certain domestication of the missionary movement in the sense that preoccupation with conquest was replaced by a sharper awareness of global problems. The essential significance of contextual variety was relativized as well. Now, the second major step in the learning process—the focus on poverty and dialogue—brings it back again. This time, however, it offers itself as a constitutive element. Contextual variety is no longer an inevitable consequence of the confrontation between a vital missionary movement and a plural world; it is the indispensable starting point for an adequate view of the interplay of the many configurations of religion, rationality, and faith, and as such for an adequate perspective on mission. It is the challenge to Western Christianity and Western theology to release themselves from their territorial captivity and to recognize the problematic nature of their relation to Western culture.

Contextuality

The term *contextuality* became a key concept in ecumenical and missionary discussion in the early 1970s when it was used to defend the right of non-Western theology to pursue a direct relation between the *missio Dei* and the historical and existential experience of its own particular situation, without submitting first to Western-based traditions. The term *contextuality* entered the discussion almost simultaneously with the emergence of black theology and liberation theology, which illustrated and confirmed the point. In these theologies, the emphasis on contextuality forces the Western partner in dialogue to become aware of the uncritical projection of presuppositions upon others and of the equally uncritical legitimation of much injustice. The message was, there can be no theology without a choice of sides.

Although contextuality became associated with a focus on social and political problems in the relation between Western and non-Western Christianity, the discussion quickly moved to the larger problem of culture and cultural plurality. For the development of Third World theology this presented a problem: for some time there was a tendency to contrast liberation theology and cultural theology, as if these had different starting points. More recent approaches try to combine both emphases. In this connection the term *inculturation* presents itself as a plausible alternative. Coined in Roman Catholic discussions, it refers to the interaction among local church, universal church, and local culture, and it draws attention to the process of the rooting of the Christian faith in a particular culture and, conversely, the enrichment of the universal church by elements of this culture.

It may be clear from this brief sketch that the terms *contextuality* and *inculturation* can easily be instrumentalized by more traditional missionary approaches that are exclusively concerned with the translation of the gospel in terms of the various cultures of the world. That is, however, not the only possibility. The terms may also help in the clarification of the complicated process by which faith is transmitted in intercultural communication and by which a particular culture receives and appropriates external messages. In that case they function similarly to the terminology proposed earlier in this essay that speaks of an interaction between configurations of religion, rationality, and faith.

Obviously, a further differentiation in terms of religion, rationality, and faith confirms and illustrates the variety of ways in which people make sense of their world contextually. Such differentiation visualizes not only the original and permanent nature of intercultural communication, but also the various ways in which mission has taken and is taking place. Missionary communication can concentrate, for instance, on the relation between faith and religion, the relation between faith and rationality, or the relation between religion and rationality—and that makes a great deal of difference for the kind of faith that eventually takes root. Likewise, the religious situation in some contexts, especially those where syncretisms and dual systems abound, defies description in traditionally confessional terms. In those contexts—for instance, in Latin America—we are confronted with a variety of configurations of religion, rationality, and faith. Terms such as "Catholic," "Protestant," and "Indigenous" begin to lose their value as classifying categories. Actually, the same can be said of the polarity between gospel and culture. The suggestion that these terms refer to realities that can be defined separately and be brought in relation with each other as two distinct entities is quite unrealistic. We are dealing with complex relations between the many forms in which gospel and culture are always intertwined already.

Against this background, the most intriguing aspect of *mission* no longer appears to be the transmission of faith from one context to another, but rather the development of faith in intercontextual communication. More precisely, transmission of faith *depends on* the potentiality of each context to forge a tenable configuration in which the Christian faith truly functions, and it *consists of* the creation of a structure of challenge and response among the various contexts. In other words, traditionally speaking, the ecumenical question overtakes and supersedes the missionary question. Transmission becomes a matter of dialogue.

It is important to underline that the concept of contextuality in modern ecumenical discussion does not refer merely to particularisms. Contextual theology, for instance, is not merely something that is developed in isolation in one particular place without any relation with the whole. The concept of contextuality includes a necessary reference to the whole, because it presupposes the problems of globalization. Contextuality refers not only to the expression of local sentiments, but it is, in combination with that, a choice of position in the problematic structure of the world, with a view toward the unity of humankind.

At this point it may be useful to remember that our analysis of secularization spoke at one point about the interreligious alliances that would be necessary in order to come to terms with the global dimensions of the Western problem of religion and rationality. Against this background, contextuality acquires the features of *protest,* and the intercontextual "structure of challenge and response" becomes the definition of an ecumenical movement that takes the problem of the unity of humankind with utmost seriousness. For such an ecumenical movement, a positive appreciation of plurality is crucial; it is a major condition for the understanding and the spreading of the gospel.

The *kairos* of the ecumenical movement is the fact that Christianity has been globalized as well. It is not only the Western problem that has assumed global dimensions. Christianity—in its historical entanglement with Western history, which cannot be ignored, and with the specifically Western problem of religion and rationality as its thorn in the flesh—has become embedded in many non-Western contexts. These contexts form the starting points for a new reflection about this Western problem, and from there a reflection about the whole of the tradition. In this reflection, traditional (Western) Christianity will be challenged to relativize its historical alliance with modern rationality and to seek new strongholds in the religious variety of humankind. Such a relativization will no doubt imply a shift from unity to plurality and fragmentation. But this will also be a shift toward a stronger anchoring in people's contextual struggle for survival and in the basic human religious search.

Secularization Revisited

The problem of secularization as analyzed in this essay requires a reformulation of the goals, means, and motives of mission. Beyond that, it requires a rethinking of the position of Christianity in a religiously and culturally plural world, even a reconstruction of its tradition in that perspective. However, what is generally regarded as the Christian tradition may in hindsight be conceived as a series of efforts to do just that. In that respect, secularization only reactivates a basic missionary feature of the Christian faith, just as it reactivates the primary reality of intercultural communication. Of course, this reactivation takes place in a problematic and ambiguous way. It is accompanied by the presentation of a framework for the "unity of humankind" that is, to a large extent, indispensable, but that has its obvious destructive effects on human life in many respects. This problem is the inescapable framework in which the missionary message and presence of the Christian faith have to be reconsidered. It is the form in which reflection on the relation between God and world is bound to take place.

In terms of our analysis, it is the calling of the Christian faith to establish and reestablish bridges between the diversity of human religion on the one hand and a highly problematic global rationality on the other hand—and to do this in a convincing and relevant way. Understandably, there is the strong temptation to build these bridges out of the material of a preconceived and well-defined specific configuration of religion, rationality, and faith. This is basically the fundamentalist temptation. It remains attractive because it claims to offer a stronger alliance of faith and rationality than the one that has produced the problem of secularization. And yet in its analysis it does not go to the heart of this problem. In the end, it underestimates both the necessary power of religion and the indispensability of modern rationality. The bridge may be strong, but it is not firmly anchored in the banks it seeks to connect.

Mission, of course, is deeply concerned with the vitality and the spreading of the Christian gospel. Precisely this concern should lead to a clear recognition and a responsible and consistent analysis of the problems of today's world in relation to faith and religion. All the implications and consequences of the process of secularization will have to be taken seriously. Only when we have begun to see these implications and consequences can we begin to reflect on the possibility of a missionary revival in the context of modern Western culture itself.

5

A Conversation with Lesslie Newbigin

No one who wants to participate in the discussion on secularization and mission can afford to ignore the influential contribution of Lesslie Newbigin, who, in several publications over the last fifteen years (1983; 1986; 1989; 1991), has called attention to the marginalized and weakened position of Christian faith in modern Western culture. Having spent a lifetime as a missionary in India, he diagnoses the ills of Western culture mainly in terms of loss of direction and purpose, a narrow understanding of rationality, and immunity to the claim of the gospel. Moreover, in his view, the Christian churches have largely underestimated the basic incompatibility between Christian faith and Enlightenment thinking; accordingly, they have let themselves be taken in by basic Enlightenment assumptions, even in their theology and social ethics. In fact, according to Newbigin, they have allowed themselves to be banished to the private realm, where religion is tolerated as long as it does not interfere with the public realm of so-called objective truth. There is a need, then, for a strong missionary reassertion of the Christian faith, precisely on the basis of the *public* claim of the gospel.

This chapter intends to survey Newbigin's approach on the basis of the analysis developed in the preceding chapters.

Not all aspects of Newbigin's work will be dealt with; only a few key concepts that express the basic direction of his thinking and come close to concepts used in the preceding analysis will be highlighted.

Public Truth

According to Newbigin's description of modern Western culture, only one particular kind of truth is allowed to enter into and to dominate the realm of public discourse—that is so-called objective truth, which is interested only in facts and causes and not in purpose. Modern culture is taken captive by a rationality that refers all questions of purpose, ultimate coherence, and value to the realm of personal preference.

Newbigin's appeal for a reassertion of the Christian faith as public truth, therefore, necessarily implies a challenge to rethink this prevalent notion of objectivity. There are, in fact, two aspects to his appeal. The first is the claim that the gospel is about private *and* public life, that it contains the message of Christ's lordship over the *whole* of human existence. The community that lives from this gospel and interprets the world from this point of view can never resign itself to this modern distinction between public and private. The second is the insight, derived mainly from the philosopher of science Michael Polanyi, that a responsible search for truth will be unable to separate subjective and objective factors, believing from knowing. In other words, a public commitment to the search for truth should make room for the committed input of particular traditions and communities. Armed with this claim and this insight, Christianity should enter the realm of *public* discussion about *truth.*

The public-private distinction roughly corresponds to the distinction used in Chapter 1 between the world of self-sufficient rational systems, on the one hand, and the life-worlds, where existential encompassing choices are made and where life is perceived and experienced as a coherent whole, on the other. This latter distinction, however, implies a constant struggle or competition between a colonizing tendency of the systems and assertions of meaning and identity on the part of the life-worlds. The role of religion is not a foregone conclusion in this analysis, except for the point that one of its traditional functions—the integration of scattered life-worlds into one framework—has become obsolete. Functional rationality has made such integration impossible.

Does Newbigin mean this integration when he speaks about the reentry of religion, more specifically the Christian faith, into the public realm? That would imply a return to some version of theocracy or Christian establishment. Newbigin has always denied that this is his intention; but in his work it does not become unambiguously clear. He elaborates the public function of Christian faith along two different lines, which we might call the "Augustine" and the "Bonhoeffer" lines. Along the first line, Newbigin argues that trinitarian and incarnational thinking should be the controlling public truth. This thinking created a new foundation for culture in Augustine's day, when all other systems were breaking down, and it may do the same thing today. It offers itself as an "inclusive rationality," which can retain the great achievements of modern culture and at the same time restore them into the necessary framework of value and purpose. Along the second line, Newbigin refers to the protest of the German Confessing Church against the Nazi regime. The point here is the unmasking of ideologies, using the dual method of affirmation and anathema. The church has to make clear where it stands when the integrity of the gospel is *publicly* at stake.

Both lines converge in Newbigin's insistence that a responsible church in a responsible society "enters vigorously into the struggle for truth in the public domain" and proclaims the gospel "as part of the continuing conversation which shapes public doctrine" (1991:59, 64), thus choosing a middle road between theocracy and agnostic pluralism. But some confusion remains. Should Christian faith aspire to occupy the "central shrine of society," which is and should be empty, according to Michael Novak? Or should it present itself in the form of a permanent *status confessionis,* a permanent prophetic reminder of the sickness of modern culture? And then also, are these the only alternatives to the so-called privatization? Could it not be that privatization of religion does not by definition exclude various other forms of creative public influence? It seems that the all-too-rigid distinction between public and private that Newbigin uses prevents him from developing this point with more flexibility. It is all or nothing for him.

The difficulty lies in the fact that Newbigin deals with faith as an alternative rationality, placing it on one level and in competition with public rationality, and involving it in a battle for truth. He does not go into the complexities of the relation between faith and rationality that we have tried to trace in Chapter 2. The main complexities are, first, that modern (functional) rationality has severed its original connections with religion and, second, that faith without religion is a head without a body. In other words, to concentrate exclusively on the function of Christian faith as an overarching explanatory discourse, as a new starting point for thought about the totality of human experience, would be to ignore one of the main problems of secularization and to opt for a shortcut. It is far from clear that we have two forms of truth here that can meaningfully be placed on one level of competition. Does functional rationality imply a truth that can be compared with the truth of a *faith*? Newbigin asserts as much, with the aid of the concept of "plausibility structure." He insists that what has come to function as public truth is in fact just another plausibility structure, *like the Christian faith.*

Attractive though this position is, it overlooks certain things. For instance, functional rationality has emancipated itself from the debate of faiths, and its success has depended precisely on this emancipation. For Christian faith to compete with this success is to give up the possibility of counteracting the destructive effects of the Western problem. In other words, the public role of the gospel has to be constructed along different lines.

What Newbigin finds most difficult to accept, it seems, is the plurality of plausibility structures, with functional rationality taking the place of what was once an integrating center. He calls this repeatedly the "nightmare of subjectivism and relativism." He does not appreciate that this plurality is the scene of many existential struggles, many choices for meaning and identity, in which fact and value are permanently intertwined. The central shrine has been replaced with something much more creative. The public world of modern Western culture is not only the rigidly dogmatic world of so-called objective facts—although it is that, too, and it may become even more so when we let the process of secularization run its course. It is also a common arena of discourse, created by an emancipated rationality for the sake of the survival of the human community. As such it is very different from the public world of Augustine's time, and also from whatever *public* means in the gospel. These differences should not be overlooked when we reflect on the gospel as public truth.

Two Rationalities

For Newbigin, the problem of Christian faith and modern culture presents itself as a clear choice. Shall we consider the Bible from the point of view of the dominant culture, or the other way around? There are two plausibility structures here: one that surrenders to the biases of public, objective reasoning, and one that is forthrightly confessional. To be sure, the Christian faith can be explained in both ways, but obviously only one is adequate from a missionary point of view.

Newbigin's view of modern Western philosophy is quite uncomplicated. The rationality of the Enlighten-ment is basically anti-Christian. Descartes is a blind alley. The Cartesian starting point in fundamental doubt is "a small-scale repetition of the Fall" (1991:27). The quest for certainty and for a sure foundation of knowledge leads only to further questioning and to an infinite regress, unless faith becomes the starting point. Without faith as the starting point for rationality, without revelation becoming the basis for reasoning, we have no defense against Nietzsche, for whom the basic factor in the quest for truth was the will to power.

Here again we encounter Newbigin's fundamental fear of pluralism and open-ended discussion. Behind this fear is a deep concern for the modern Western human being, as well as for the integrity of the gospel. However, to construct a fundamental antithesis between Christian faith and Enlightenment is questionable, not only from a historical point of view, but also theologically. Faith and rationality have grown up together in the history of Western culture, in close entanglement. There have been tensions from the first alliance between Christian believing and Greek thinking, but also much mutual dependence and benefit. In this history, the Enlightenment is both result and symptom of a fundamental problem of Western culture, in which all efforts to interpret the gospel and to formulate the faith have participated almost by definition. It would be artificial to separate the two and to suggest that Christianity can be presented as an alternative rationality.

Nevertheless, this is what Newbigin wants. That is why the Enlightenment has to become the scapegoat. In the process, however, three basic points are overlooked. First, Newbigin underestimates the degree to which faith itself is part of the problem, an accomplice in the development of a culture that produced the Enlightenment, and is unable to dispose of the Enlightenment in its inescapable rational functions. Faith cannot be rescued and purged from a complex history of configurations of religion, rationality, and faith. Second, he also underestimates the degree to which the Enlightenment has been an ally of the Christian faith. It has stimulated Christianity to develop and refine its view of universal history and of eschatology. Even though Newbigin is undoubtedly right when he draws attention to basic incompatibilities in regard to the concept of history, there is more than just opposition here. Third, when faith is presented as another species of rationality, it almost automatically follows that the problematic aspects of rationality, the points where it elicits contradiction and protest because it tends to neglect and violate essential aspects of human life, remain underexposed. In Newbigin's case it implies that he concentrates much more on the battle for truth than on the struggles for justice and liberation, which have revealed the dark sides of the history of rationality. And it is precisely on those dark sides that faith has to come to life again. Its major business is not the rational fight against modern unbelief but the exposure of the crisis of rationality with regard to full humanity. Newbigin would reply that both are necessary and that the second task can be performed adequately only after the first has been dealt with. Basically, however, they present different preoccupations that may ultimately work at cross-purposes.

All this is not to deny that the Enlightenment, more specifically the later development of functional rationality, presents serious problems to the integrity of a Christian faith that seeks to maintain itself in this context. But Newbigin's approach of early and massive polarization must be regarded as an inadequate reaction to these problems, for it underestimates their complexity and leads to the neglect of vital challenges in the contemporary world situation.

The Logic of Mission

Fundamental to Newbigin's approach to the problem of Christianity and culture is, of course, his understanding of the gospel. In his view, a vigorous missionary attitude is a logical consequence of faith, for the gospel focuses on the appearance of Christ as the key event for the understanding of the whole of human history. This one particular event elucidates the whole of reality. The "scandal of particularity" is the most important element in Newbigin's biblical theology (Newbigin 1978). It is understandable from this that one of Newbigin's major missionary disputes is with concepts of universal history that absorb individual events as mere passing instances or at most as illustrations of the whole. His quarrel with Hinduism is, in this respect, quite similar to his quarrel with Enlightenment thinking. Neither can appropriate the Christ event as the key. This is why the logic of mission requires an outright and fundamental opposition to both cultures. For Newbigin, it also requires opposition to much modern liberal theology, insofar as it has surrendered this basic point and developed Christologies without *skandalon,* without conversion, and without public claims.

The scandal of particularity is, for Newbigin, identical with the mystery of divine election. In his exposition of this fundamental insight, he emphasizes that election is not just the designation of an individual or a people as something special, but that it implies a chain of communication. Election is basically missionary in the sense that it is itself a witness and should take the form of witness. The particularity of election, then, is the particularity of a history in which the non-elect become part of the story. From Israel this history moves toward the Gentiles, and from there back to Israel. Particularity is the inclusion of *the others* in an ongoing movement, centered in the particularity of Christ. This is the logic of mission.

There is much in this approach that is theologically valuable. However, in line with the preceding sections of this chapter, it must also be noted that the approach tends to be formal and abstract. The particularity itself tends to become the message, rather than the way in which it presents itself as relevant to particular contexts of struggle. *That* Christ is the key tends to become more important than *the way in which* he is the key. Newbigin's biblical theology in *The Open Secret* begins with the notions of authority and commitment, and it presents Jesus as the man with *exousia,* without showing how these notions are related to a specific history of temptation and choice and of human interrelatedness. It is the same problem we had in relation to the claim to public truth: it is as it were an a priori claim; it is not presented and explained in the context of specific struggles and inculturation processes. It is presented as coming from outside, as a challenge to thinking. It is at this point that Newbigin's approach manifests both its strength and its weakness.

Secularization Revisited

It is obvious and also understandable that Newbigin's strong appeal to reassert Christian faith in defiance of the blind alleys of modern Western culture meets with much positive response. There is a clarity about it that makes it attractive in a context full of ambivalence and uncertainty. Believers and church leaders who suffer under the primary and more ephemeral aspects of the secularization process—the decline of public influence of Christian faith, the decline of church membership, the loss of direction in Christian education—are likely to respond to it with new enthusiasm. They are also likely to accept the implication that it is Christianity's own fault that modern culture has become what it is: Christians have by and large failed to show missionary strength. They are called to make up for that now.

In our review of Newbigin's challenge, one of the persistent implicit questions has been whether his analysis of secularization is adequate. The answer must be: yes, insofar as it articulates and reflects on the experience of tension between public and private, between system and life-world; no, insofar as it stops too soon and does not raise questions about the ambivalence of rationality as such and about the permanent precariousness of the balance between religion, rationality, and faith. Yes, insofar as it calls Christianity to reflect seriously on its position in modern culture; no, insofar as this call focuses exclusively on the battle for truth between two rationalities, and thereby feeds an omnipresent nostalgia for an influential Christian establishment or a widely convincing *status confessionis,* in which ideologies are beaten by faith.

Perhaps the main difference between Newbigin's analysis of secularization and mine is that the former focuses on the revitalization of Christian faith as such, over against the threats and temptations of modern rationality, whereas the latter focuses on the global problems created by modern rationality in the world of cultures and religions, and on the necessity to restore or at least counteract this rationality for the sake of a true unity of humankind. A missionary revitalization of Christian faith is considered to be essential also in the latter analysis; but here this revitalization needs to be carefully considered and constructed in the perspective of the wider problem.

Theologically, the difference between the two analyses might be stated as follows. For Newbigin, the gospel presents us with a clear *worldview,* centered in the Christ event, and in need of interpretation, formulation, and institutionalization in and, if necessary, over against all cultures. For me, the gospel speaks of judgment and promise, exemplified once and for all in the Christ event, and in need of recognition and reinterpretation in the tensions and conflicts of human history. Revelation cannot be institutionalized as public faith; it is present in the form of an eschatological question and a challenge to reorder our configurations of religion, rationality, and faith in its perspective.

A public affirmation of the gospel against the background of a complete and sustained analysis of the process of secularization can only take the form of a serious involvement in the complex business of balancing religion, rationality, and faith. Otherwise it will run the risk of remaining artificial and rhetorical and of tempting people to believe in uncritical reproductions of their tradition. And it will not solve, but will rather reinforce, the problem of the relation between faith and rationality. In other words, it will run the risk of coming close to fundamentalism. Fundamentalism is also one of the pitfalls Newbigin seeks to avoid, together with relativism. But can it be avoided in the long run, with his diagnosis and his therapy?

6

Mission: Vitality and Coherence

At the end of Chapter 4 it was suggested that the secularization process reactivates a basic missionary feature of the Christian faith, just as it reactivates the primary reality of intercultural communication. This implies that the secularization problem is the inescapable framework in which the missionary message and presence of the Christian faith will have to be reconsidered. It provokes further reflection on the relation between God and the world.

These suggestions underscore the importance of mission and the missionary movement for the self-understanding of Christianity in the contemporary world. Contrary to what it is still largely taken to be—an exotic and peripheral concern for the conversion of people of other faiths and cultures—its experiences and insights, especially with regard to de-territorialization and intercultural communication, are of vital importance in dealing with the issues of secularization. For a serious involvement in the complex business of balancing religion, rationality, and faith, and of establishing and reestablishing bridges between religion and rationality in a convincing and relevant way, even in the context of Western culture, these experiences and insights are most valuable.

To what extent can such an involvement be called mission; in what sense can the traditional and tested meanings of the word *mission* be related to the problems created by modern rationality in the world of cultures and religions, and to the necessity of restoring or at least counteracting this rationality for the sake of a true unity of humankind? This is the leading question of this last chapter. It seeks a theological interpretation of mission that is continuous with the best insights of the missionary movement, and that responds adequately to the predicament in which this movement finds itself today.

Testing the Story

The complex plurality of faith stories cannot be reduced to a clean competition of truths, for the simple reason that this plurality is part of an even more complex network of interactions between religion and rationality. Dialogue and communication between people of various cultures and religions on various levels and in various forms, therefore, have to be considered under the aspect of this problem, and of their function in the global tension between life-world and rational system. It is in this tension that various configurations of religion, rationality, and faith are designed and tried out, both individually and collectively, even on the level of nations and religions. The battle of these configurations is the stuff of culture and of intercultural communication. It is a permanent battle because of the absence of any sustainable unity of humankind, and it is reactivated by the process of secularization. This reactivation implies that new configurations emerge again and again in particular settings. In this sense, the complex interaction between configurations has eschatological significance; it reaches out to some encompassing and reconciling unity and truth.

The confrontation of humankind with the story of the Christian gospel inevitably takes place in this context; it is part of the permanent interaction between people, communities, and cultures in which different configurations challenge and inspire each other to critical self-investigation. This means that the gospel is tried out and tested in a common search for sustainable forms of human life (salvation) and that critical questions are raised in both directions.

The reactivation of global communication that is presupposed here is not at all self-evident. Defensive reactions against secularization and against the threat of intercultural diversity tend to block and frustrate communication everywhere. Mission—the confrontation of humankind with the story of the Christian gospel—cannot function in such situations of noncommunication, although sometimes it is itself understood and practiced as a defensive reaction. Conversely, as long as mission seeks to retain its eschatological dimension—true to the tradition of the missionary movement—it necessarily presupposes and includes the encouragement of open communication. Perhaps the worldwide discipling of people means precisely this—keeping the process of eschatological communication going through the story of Jesus.

That is not the same thing as saying that mission aims at the reproduction of particular versions of this story in other contexts. Such a formulation tends to gloss over too many complexities. It might be more adequate to say that mission is the encouragement of processes of communication in which the gospel gets a chance to function as the basis of people's effort to construct meaning and coherence in their lives. As indicated before, this means that the primary missionary problem is not conveyance, adaptation, translation, and understanding of a given form of faith, but rather, development of contextual faith. And this, in turn, means trying out ways in which the gospel story can help to structure and reinterpret forms of human religion with a view to enabling people to cope with alienating yet indispensable forms of rationality.

A Key Metaphor

Of course, this is only a first step in the reconsideration of
what mission might mean. The next obvious question is,
what exactly is it that mission wants to communicate, and
on what grounds is this claimed to be indispensable for
human salvation? Serious reflection on mission will try to
avoid the pitfall of saying that the gospel story is just as
good as any other story that fosters intercultural communication in the sense described above; it will also need to
avoid the pitfall of presenting one particular configuration
of religion, rationality, and Christian faith as the solution
for the whole of humankind.

One of the most difficult issues in the whole area of mission, dialogue, and plurality is the possibility of formulating
the basic thrust of the Christian gospel in a way that is general enough to preclude its identification with a particular
cultural system, and at the same time specific enough to
make it distinct and recognizable. Such a formulation is
not to be sought for the sake of having one general authoritative point of reference in intercontextual communication, but for the sake of expressing what sort of dynamic
mission seeks to encourage. A summary of the fundamental truths of the Christian faith, useful though it might be,
cannot fulfill this function, because it aims at elucidating
and structuring an already developed contextual faith. A
selection of the most important stories of Scripture, or
even a general outline of the gospel, cannot fulfill this function, because these are the stuff of missionary communication and themselves provoke the meta-question as to what
end they serve and why they are claimed to be important
for human beings. What is needed, rather, is a formulation
that can be recognized in different contexts as a pacesetter
of inculturation, as a metaphor that activates further creative rearticulation of the faith. The metaphor should be
able to stimulate both personal spirituality and community

building; it should refer to important aspects of the Christian tradition and at the same time lead people past fixed positions toward further reflection. Above all, it should express the power of the gospel to deal with the ever-present challenge of the unity of humankind, in which universality and particularity are no longer mutually exclusive.

At the end of Chapter 3 it was suggested that unity of humankind requires the art of combining two apparently contradictory projects. One is bringing together peoples, nations, and races in an effective and efficient system of communication that produces and promotes justice. The other is taking seriously peoples, nations, and races in their genuine particularity, their distinctiveness. Guided by this formulation, we might try to summarize the basic thrust of the gospel in the twin terms *gathering* and *multiplying,* and continue to strengthen this proposal by the following considerations.

First, *gathering* and *multiplying* are fundamentally biblical terms; they combine the covenant between God and God's people, of the kingdom and its justice with the plurality of all nations and all people. The essential tension between Jew and Gentile is expressed in them. Second, the terms are clearly not propositional summaries or messages; rather, they draw attention to the fact that summaries and messages and stories, indispensable as they are, function to illustrate, support, and flesh out the ongoing construction of meaning on the basis of the gospel. Third, the first term of the metaphor, *gathering,* suggests a sustained effort to establish complete humanization, opposing all religious and political power that stands in its way; the second term, *multiplying,* suggests the unlimited acceptance of human beings as they are. Their dynamic thus turns against the violence that seeks uniformity, and against the violence that seeks fragmentation; it presupposes the hope that a sustainable combination of unity and diversity, of justice and plurality, might yet be possible.

*Mission, we might summarize, is the reproduction and
the encouragement of the dynamic of gathering and multiplying present in the proclamation of Jesus.*

The presentation of this key metaphor does not imply a
proposal for a summary of the Christian faith. It is merely
an example that can be replaced and complemented by
others of the direction in which we might move when dealing with the issue of generality and specificity. If it intends
to summarize anything, it is the missionary presupposition
of any formulation of the faith, or even (if it is permissible
to use this worn-out concept) of the *missio Dei*—the preceding active presence of God in summarizing and bringing
together all reality in Christ. At the same time, it is meant
to place mission in the context of the problem of secularization that we have tried to analyze and to draw attention
to two further aspects of mission that come to light as soon
as this context is taken seriously.

The first is the affinity of mission to political activity.
The proposed key metaphor brings mission very close to
the problems that have their origin in the process of secularization and display their effects in countless lives and
contexts throughout the world. At the same time, the
metaphor is not merely a statement of liberation; it is full
of eschatological references; it speaks of a promise to be
fulfilled by God, yet present as a permanent challenge.

The second aspect is the affinity of mission to the reality of pluralism. The proposed key metaphor draws attention to the necessity of giving theological significance to
pluralism, rather than just accepting it as inevitable. It
reminds the Christian faith of its indebtedness to the
uniquely Jewish insight that God is to be known and
encountered in historical experience, rather than in universal ideas. The appropriation of this insight by Christian
faith does not mean that particularity is replaced by universality, although it has often been presented in that way.
It means, rather, that the particularity of knowledge of and

encounter with God is reproduced again and again, until the ends of the earth, and it implies that Christ has become the key event that expresses the possibility and the promise of this reproduction.

Salvation for Humankind

A reconsideration of the meaning of mission in the perspective of an analysis of worldwide secularization and pluralism will ultimately have to face the question in what sense the Christian gospel can be called universally valid and necessary for the salvation of humankind. Even if proclamation of the gospel is understood in terms of the development of contextual faith, subject to a permanent process of intercultural communication with an eschatological view to a unity of humankind that unites truth, justice, and reconciliation in a final way—even then the question remains: is there one fundamental message that encompasses the whole?

On the level of testing the story, the answer is that the testing simply continues; that universal validity of the gospel is assumed until the evidence contradicts the assumption; and that as long as there are people and communities that work with this story. There is no necessity of a priori claims here, only the ongoing engagement in communication. On the level of the key metaphor, the answer is that the basic thrust of the gospel responds to basic needs and problems of humankind; that there may be other stories with different thrusts and different analyses of needs and problems; but that as long as people in different cultures recognize the validity of this approach it can claim to be at least universally significant.

The answers are important, but they still fall short of the traditional claim that the Christian mission, however it conceives its task, confronts the world with the *only* way in which it can find coherence and salvation. There is, in the traditions of the Christian faith, a prophetic insistence that what is conveyed here is somehow the final word. What is left of that insistence in our reconsideration?

The problem here is the relation between two different levels of speaking about mission. The first level speaks about communication, contextuality, plurality, change, conversion in an ongoing open-ended history of humankind. The second level speaks about proclamation, ultimate truth, final choice. Both are essential, but their combination is problematic. If the two levels are simply connected in an uncritical way or even allowed to coincide, absolutism appears. If they are left unrelated or even separated, relativism appears. The middle course is called *pneumatology;* it refers to the Holy Spirit as the active link between the two levels.

Speaking about the Spirit in the Christian tradition has always served the purpose of combining the once-for-all character of the Christ event with the partial, broken, relative, and yet inspiring and life-giving appropriations of this event in human history. In terms of our analysis so far, the Spirit activates human (intercultural) communication, it keeps bringing this communication back to the original form of gathering and multiplying, and it inspires people to speak about salvation for humankind. These three lines belong together, not as parts of a doctrine that functions in the way of an ideology, but as aspects of a spirituality that encourages people to move ahead together, a spirituality that is characterized by guilt and forgiveness and that keeps the eschatological unity of truth, justice, and reconciliation permanently before the world. It is a spirituality that enables people to recognize new and different forms of faith, new and different configurations of religion, rationality, and faith, as challenges to find new ways to express the basic thrust of the gospel and to rethink and reinterpret its tradition. It is a spirituality that stages the permanent (eschatological) conflict between self-alienation and salvation.

Final truth is not the truth of a one-sidedly pressed particular conviction; it is, rather, a truth about human communication itself. Christian faith is the proleptic formulation of such a truth, which means that it is itself subject to the processes of communication even as it seeks to keep these processes open toward their eschatological fulfillment.

Secularization Revisited

We return once more to the analysis of secularization as presented earlier. One of the main theses of this analysis was that the human search for truth and direction can be formulated in terms of a search for balance between religion, rationality, and faith; that the Western problem implies that these balances are generally threatened and upset; and that there is a particular need to re-anchor faith in the plurality of forms in which human religion is expressed.

Religion, in our definition, includes the longing for wholeness of the world of humanity and the world of nature, as well as the protest against a rationality that produces death and threatens humanity and nature. Although religion needs the further structuring and protection of faith—in order to resist the temptation to build a universe of its own without interaction with public rationality—precisely these elements are essential for the correction and broadening of a narrow rational conception of the unity of humankind. Rationality, on the other hand, presents important and necessary limits to the range of action of religion. One cannot just go back to before the Enlightenment, and human society needs to check the tendencies to incoherence and chaos that are also present in religion. Nevertheless, the modern Western alliance between faith and rationality shows that the Christian faith has generally defined itself one-sidedly on the basis of these limits and checks, rather than on the basis of the longing and protest of religion. New alliances of faith with precisely these religious sources, in their pluriform presence throughout the world, might contribute to the redemption of rationality, its liberation from its dead alleys.

The permanent and universal struggle of life-worlds against the idols of death has eschatological significance. This struggle should not be conceived in a dualistic manner, but as directed toward the conversion of rationality. Precisely at this point the power and the dialogical value of the Christian faith should continue to be tested. Such testing involves the transformation and restructuring of much religion, even when this religion has become part of other faiths and rationalities. This testing produces new bridges, new contextual forms of faith.

The alternative to this reconception of mission remains, of course, fundamentalism. It is, in a sense, a plausible alternative. In its own way, it takes the threats of secularization and modern functional rationality seriously. Nonetheless, it is unable to appreciate the theological significance of pluralism; ultimately, its alternative rationality is just as suspicious of religion as the rationality it combats. Consequently, its faith can only be the reproduction of particular idealized configurations. As suggested in the course of this essay, the temptation of fundamentalism, conceived in this way, is much more widely present than in what is technically called fundamentalism. Any reconception of mission in the perspective of worldwide secularization that is intent upon avoiding the pitfalls of both absolutism and relativism should recognize it as a temptation, and accordingly resist it.

A Conversation with Bert Hoedemaker

Charles C. West

From now on, therefore, we regard no one from a
human point of view; even though we once regarded
Christ from a human point of view, we regard him
thus no longer. Therefore, if any one is in Christ
[there] is a new creation; the old has passed away,
behold, the new has come.

2 Cor. 5:16–17

Missiology is a discipline that is wonderfully free of limits
and controls. Any content that pertains to God's work
through human agents is subject matter for it; any method
that brings order to this content can be a valid instrument
of its research. Professor Hoedemaker, in his essay
"Secularization and Mission," makes full use of this freedom. His basic method is sociological with, as is the case
with all substantive sociology, philosophical definitions and
reflections woven in. His aim, however, is to influence theology, particularly that theology that guides the way the
church presents its message amid the plural forms of
faith, rationality, and religion in a secularized world. This
approach produces a helpful critique and a great many
insights that practitioners of mission may use. The question is, What might happen to the analysis and the pre-
scription he offers if theology, not sociology, were the
controlling discipline?

One must begin, however, with an effort to understand the essay from its own point of view. There is risk in this; clarification may bring misunderstanding, and meaning may be lost. But this, too, is part of the dialogue. Hoedemaker defines secularization by describing it throughout his essay, but three other concepts—rationality, religion, and faith—provide the structure for understanding it. Rationality he defines as "the human capacity to organize and understand, to apply logical connections to a seemingly chaotic world, to establish communication according to accepted rules, and to cultivate things according to preconceived plans." Religion "refers to the human preoccupation with finitude, failure, suffering, the encounter of good and evil, the experience of love and anxiety. [It] is the constant struggle with radical contingency. The struggle expresses itself primarily in a loose variety of activities and ideas that might be characterized as symbolic-ritual." Faith is "the structuring of 'religious' activities by way of a tradition, a community, a story, a 'truth,' or a revelation." It is the bridge between religion and rationality. The tension of these three elements is perennial in culture. Culture is healthiest when they are in balance. In recent centuries, however, secularization has thrown this balance off. Rationality, having been generated by religion, developed its own systems of explanation, control, and action—Hoedemaker names the political and the economic but implies also the scientific and technological—which, by their coherent power, reduced religion to a private optional sphere of human experience. More recently, these systems have lost their coherence with one another and become various structures of "functional rationality," but still they exercise organizing managerial power on a global scale. Religion, meanwhile, now recognizing itself in its plural forms across the world and therefore no longer only as Christian, struggles to develop faith systems that will give form to the sense of social and cosmic "life force" that its various cultures feel, thereby helping them to resist the secularization that modern functional rationality forces on them.

Thus Hoedemaker the sociologist. He is more than this, however. A serious philosophical humanism guides him in offering prescriptions and projecting goals. Faith systems, he says, can move toward fundamentalism, a somewhat unclear concept that suggests a socially divisive but internally coherent rational structure of faith that resists modern secularization but at the same time falls victim to its basic functional method. Or faiths can develop an "eschatologically open" global dialogue that seeks the unity of humankind through "interfaith alliances"—"an effective and efficient system of communication that produces and promotes justice" while at the same time "taking seriously people, nations, and races in their genuine particularity." This is Hoedemaker's hope: that a functional imperative to which even faith is instrumental will produce a vision of communicative interaction open to the promise of a new saving reality that will emerge out of the communication itself. This is also the way, he believes, Christian mission should go; not "the transmission of faith from one context to another, but rather the development of faith in intercontextual communication." He aims to prove Jürgen Habermas wrong to exclude religion from his "theory of communicative action"; but he adopts the model and method of Habermas's proposal and raises its modest hope to a higher, religious power.

There is also another, more explicitly Christian, motif in Hoedemaker's essay. But before we come to it, let us examine the route traveled so far. Where does it lead us to define rationality, faith, and religion as he does and to explain secularization with these tools of understanding?

Rationality

First, it is not surprising that having defined rationality functionally, Hoedemaker ends up discerning that, in modern society, it is largely functional. He has a point, to be sure, over against Lesslie Newbigin whom he criticizes, that rational truth claims today present themselves not in terms of one massive system of human reason, but rather plural "plausibility structures" corresponding to various fields of human thought and activity, most of which claim to be only useful and effective, not universally valid. What he neglects is the history of this rationality and the interaction of divine revelation with it.

This is a long history; only a few critical points need be mentioned here. In the first place, rationality, at least in its Greek and Chinese origins, was profoundly metaphysical. It was an effort by the human mind to discern the order of the universe and to attune human life to it. Its relation to religion depends on definition. It interacted with mythology, with divinity, and with concepts of human life and destiny in various ways. In a broad sense, it *was* religious—the order of the human mind reflecting in the universe the mind of God—although in some tension (as Hoedemaker recognizes) with more symbolic and emotional expressions of religious "life force."

Many efforts were made by the Greek and Latin Fathers of the Church to capture the metaphysic of Greek and Roman philosophy for biblical truth, with varying results. Most influential in forming the modern mind was medieval Thomist philosophy, which gave "natural" reason a positive relation to divinely revealed truth about human destiny and the fulfillment of all things. The image of God was found in human rationality. It was seen as a direct way of perceiving universal truth up to a certain level, needing only perfection, not revision, by divine revelation. Enlightenment, confidence in human reason and natural law, was a continuation of this faith, without divine revelation or the authority of the church.

Rationality in this sense, however, played only a peripheral role in the history of God with the covenant people, in the Old Testament or the New. Wisdom and knowledge, rooted in the fear of the Lord, were a differently motivated use of the human mind. They aimed at understanding the character of the covenant and behind it the character of a just and merciful God. In this context the people of God explored human relations, the wonders of creation, and the promise of the coming messiah, by way of repentance and renewal. It came to a focus in the Crucified, "folly to the [nations *(ethné)*], but to those who are called, both Jews and Greeks, Christ the power of God and the wisdom of God" (1 Cor. 1:23–24). It involves a continual sensitivity to God's action, which changes us and the world. "Do not be conformed to this world but be transformed by the renewal of your mind, that you may prove what is the will of God, what is good and acceptable and perfect" (Rom. 12:2).

This biblical perspective has provided an antimetaphysical countermovement throughout Western history. The Reformers all understood truth as relational in the biblical sense and found reason to be as sinful and corrupt as any other part of self-centered human nature. The justification of the sinful human mind by grace alone liberated that mind to explore the phenomena of nature and human behavior without fear lest the metaphysical unity of truth be broken. In this sense, Reformed theology was the (not always conscious) ancestor both of the empirical method in scientific investigation and of the functional rationality that Hoedemaker describes in the postmodern world. On the other hand, these same Reformers made the world more aware of the corruption of reason by human sins of pride, greed, self-interest, and lust for power. They were the ancestors also of modern sensitivity to ideology that calls itself science and to the bias of special interest in all systems of political and economic reasoning.

The heart of the matter is that rationality, in Christian perspective, is *relational.* It is rooted in a commitment to the other in the relation, which is personal and is usually known (though not by Hoedemaker) as faith. This is the force of Newbigin's argument. Hoedemaker reaches for this insight in his advocacy of communication, but he misses its full implications. Reason operates in the context of self-and-other, even in investigating the physical world (Michael Polanyi). How much more in the human context! Functional rationality contains a Christian insight, over against its Enlightenment predecessor: that all truth is limited and distorted by the particular relational context that it explores, explains, and guides. But functional rationality rejects the other as meaningless, when that other lies outside its context.

Hoedemaker seeks justice and the unity of the world through communicative rationality across contexts. He includes religious contexts. This is good. But alliances and even covenants among nations and systems are not new in history. World trade is a form of communicative rationality—perhaps the only successful one in the world today—and also a field of conflict and exploitation. Science and technology, in their various interacting systems, expand common human knowledge and control, and also become the instruments of one interest against another. Even cultures and religions interpenetrate, sometimes for peace and sometimes for war. Any combination of these might produce the unity of the world—or its destruction. What Other (other reality, or God) is there, that can communicate with us and that can undergird communicative rationality?

Religion

This brings us to the other pole of humanity. What is religion? Sociologists and anthropologists have great difficulty defining it, because no definition seems quite inclusive enough. They are aware that there are experiences and activities in a culture that are not "rational" in any self-contained way, that point beyond themselves to some other reality. But there is no way, given the humanist premises of the sociological method, to explore that reality. Those who try, restrict it and usually show their bias in favor of one philosophy of religion or another.

Hoedemaker's definition, "the constant struggle with radical contingency," is about as modestly inclusive as can be and still retain any defining power. He seems to regard it as a basic urge in human life. It gives rise to faith and rational systems but is never captured by them. It is pre-rational, but somehow expressive of a culture's search for the wholeness of life against divisive forces.

The problem with this is the category itself. "Religion" is a modern Western concept. As Ernst Feil has shown in his detailed study *Religio* (1986), until the eighteenth century the Latin word meant a form of practice that is an appropriate response, in worship, thought, and action, to God, or earlier among the Romans, to the gods. It was never a central idea. It never dealt with the whole of the divine-human relation; that was the task of theology and ethics. Islam and Judaism were known, not as religions, but as other "laws." Only as the ultimacy of divine revelation was questioned, and Christian faith seemed to need validation by standards of human reason and experience, did religion emerge as the overall category of which Christianity was one expression. Despite the valiant efforts of Friedrich Schleiermacher and Paul Tillich, among others, to capture it for Christian apologetics, the category does not fit. Nor does it work for the other great faiths of humankind. The word has been imposed on Judaism, Islam, Hinduism, Buddhism, and the rest, by Western scholars, but the implied relativization of their ways of worship and belief would be rejected by them all. Each demands to be respected in its own integrity as a perception of, and response to, reality in all its dimensions, divine and human.

Still, the case can be made that there *is* something like religion, in the modern sense of the term. It is a human phenomenon, reaching beyond the self yet self-centered as all human experience is. It embodies a yearning for God, however conceived, and at the same time the construction of gods in various human images. Reinhold Niebuhr, in Christian terms, puts it thus: "It is this capacity of self-transcendence which gives rise both to the yearning after God and to the idolatrous worship of false gods. It leads both to the expectation of Christ and to the expectation of the false Christ who will vindicate us but not our neighbor" (Niebuhr 1943:65). This is universally human. It has happened in all societies, and in all ages, even before it was labeled "religion." The dramatists of ancient Greece wrestled with it. The folk literature of old China expressed it when official Confucianism glossed it over. Hinduism has faced it and found secularism a helpful counterweight. Courageous Muslim writers are trying to make Islam face it today. Contrary to Hoedemaker, Karl Barth's definition of human religion as "human attempts to justify and sanctify themselves before an image of God which they project by their own power and according to their own ideas" (Barth 1957:¶17) is not just a Christian problem, but a human one.

The question at issue, then, is, By what revealed reality is human religion brought to repentance for its idolatry and justified in its search? This is a question for all humanity and for all forms of human religion, even the covert forms that hide under the rubble of postmodern deconstruction.

Faith

That Hoedemaker cannot focus this question is due in part to his essentially rationalist and instrumental definition of faith. Faith is a structuring, he says repeatedly. It "refers to a system in which all aspects of reality—the ends of the earth and the end of time—are drawn into one perspective, a perspective to which believers respond with trust and loyalty, and in which they find their spiritual home." It makes religion rational by way of "a tradition, a community, a story, a truth, or a revelation." Its systemic organizing

activity is constantly questioned by basic religious experience; its claim to rationalize religion is in conflict with
modern functional rationalities. It is, in short, by
Hoedemaker's definition, a form of religious philosophy,
tending toward fundamentalism when it becomes too
coherent.

But this identifies faith with doctrine, relation to God
with propositions about God. There is some excuse for this
in the history of every tradition. Christians have always
wrestled with the relation between *fides qua* and *fides
quae creditur,* to use Anselm's distinction. Jews and
Muslims debate continually in similar terms about the
authority of the law. In all of these, and even among
Buddhists and Hindus, there are fundamentalists. But this
identification with systems of thought and behavior, with
doctrine or law, is a distortion. Faith is a commitment. It is
in the Bible first an adjective that means "reliable" or
"steadfast," confident in the relationship to which one is
committed. Believers do not respond with trust and loyalty to "a perspective"; they respond to God. Faith does not
set out to organize and interpret religious intuitions and
activities; it explores the mystery of God's self-communi-
cation and tries to understand humanity, the world, and
history in the light of it. The faithful bear witness to their
God in theology, worship, ethics, and mission. They do so
by pointing to the revealed mystery to which they respond,
but which they do not control.

Therefore faith is not the bridge between religion and
rationality; it is the source of both, and both are fallible,
sinful human efforts to embody the revealed reality toward
which faith points. Behind all three terms is the self-com-
munication of an ultimate other who reveals to us what we
could not, in our sin and fallibility, discover or symbolize by
ourselves. Our rationality, our sensitivity to what is right and
good, our creative imagination, and, by the way, also our religion, grow out of and bear witness to our commitment to

this relationship that has grasped us, and they are all continually corrected and given new direction by it.

Here is where Hoedemaker's basic difference with Newbigin lies. He recognizes the continual judgment of God on any historical claim to realize the divine reign. "Revelation," he writes, "cannot be institutionalized as public faith; it is present in the form of an eschatological question and a challenge to reorder our configurations of religion, rationality, and faith." But he cannot accept divine revelation in Christ and the biblical story as a living determinant of the human consciousness and of the history of human-kind. Therefore he can refer faith only to "religion" and to other human "faiths" for transformation and renewal. He finds Newbigin's faith abstract and rationalistic, because he muffles the concrete word to which Newbigin is responding. The initiator of "contextual communication" is tuned out of the dialogue.

This has its consequences for Hoedemaker's analysis of mission history. The faults that he discerns there—globalism, christological triumphalism, imposed Western traditions, dependence on modern rationality, insensitivity to the plurality of cultures, a pattern of institutional management, and, he might have mentioned, subservience to the dynamics of imperial political and economic power—are all real. Disturbing is his failure to recognize the way in which world mission in the twentieth century ecumenical movement has been awakened to these problems by the biblical message itself in the life of the church, and has integrated a process of repentance and renewal into its ongoing witness. Arend van Leeuwen in *Christianity in World History* (1964) a generation ago saw this clearly and helped us all to discern the dynamic of the *missio Dei* judging and transforming the world's dynamic in a secularizing age. The world has changed since then. The challenge of other messianic faiths has faded. The hope of revolution has soured. Functional rationalities and plural cultures, tied to economic and political powers do, indeed, as Hoedemaker discerns, characterize our time. The gospel does need to be rediscovered in context; but the context is dual: the biblical Christ and our secularities in all their plural forms.

Mission

In his final chapter, Hoedemaker seems to recognize all this. He speaks of "the confrontation of humankind with the story of the Christian gospel," or the story of Jesus. Mission is "the encouragement of processes of communication in which the gospel gets a chance to function as the basis of people's efforts to construct meaning and coherence in their lives." The basic problem of this communication is to hold together the universality and the particularity of the work of God in a pattern of gathering and multiplying (or dispersing) that shows that they are not mutually exclusive. The metaphor, he points out, is biblical, both Old Testament (Genesis 11) and New (Matthew 28:16–20). Christ is at work in both directions through the Holy Spirit. New forms of faith are continually being generated in plural contexts by this and brought into community by a spirituality that "is characterized by guilt and forgiveness and that keeps the eschatological unity of truth, justice, and reconciliation permanently before the world."

He does believe, then, in the reality and power of this triune God. The final chapter of his essay moves on a different plane from the others. It could be read as a unit by itself. Why does he hold back this faith (by my definition, not his) so long? There seem to be two reasons.

First, he is deeply antagonistic to any truth claims for the Christian message that might express the rationality, the culture, the religion, or the dogma ("faith" in his terms) of a particular society, most notably the Western, rather than the reality and power of God. "Final truth," he writes,

"is not the truth of a one-sidedly pressed particular conviction; it is, rather, a truth about human communication
itself. Christian faith is the proleptic formulation of such a
truth, which means that it is itself subject to the processes of communication even as it seeks to keep these
processes open toward their eschatological fulfillment."
This is faith (my definition) and mission in a postmodern
mood, threatened by the relativism of a secularized world,
yet determined not to shut off contact with that world with
a self-consistent "fundamentalist" faith structure. We have
the gospel story. We live by it, but we make no a priori
claims for it. We test it in many contexts and let it prove its
saving validity there, being ourselves changed in our forms
of faith, rationality, and religion, in the process.

Second, Hoedemaker feels deeply the guilt of the West
that has imposed its faith, its history, its civilization and
power, on the rest of the world, but his feeling is expressed
in humanist terms, and he looks for a humanist solution,
though in Christian terms. Communication itself, with the
story of Jesus mixed in, is salvific. Other cultures and societies, once this guilt is expiated, will accept it on their own
terms—or so we hope.

Both of these concerns are important. We forget them at
our peril. But the problem and the calling of mission deep-
en them both. Sin, to begin with the second point, infects
communication itself. We may be accepted by our dialogue
partner, but we are not thereby justified. Nor is that partner
just because we are sinful. The cross is a scandal, not just to
our Christian pretensions but also to his or hers, of whatever faith or culture. Sin, furthermore, compounds itself with
power, in all our societies. We must decide how we deal with
those powers, and our decision will be a witness, a confes-
sion of faith, in Christ or in one of those powers themselves.

So also is it with the truth claims of the gospel. There is
not only relativism and diversity in the world today; there
are also competing ultimate loyalties. Faith, in the sense of

commitment to a truth, a reality, that we believe has been revealed to us and that we cannot prove but trust ourselves to, is a nearly universal dimension of human life. Michael Polanyi has demonstrated the operation of this faith in the most secular of sciences. When religious traditions such as Hinduism, which had for centuries assumed their universality, face competing claims, they also recognize the faith-basis of their worldview. There is no way, through dialogue, to relativize these commitments. They can be replaced only by a new faith, perhaps a syncretism, perhaps a conversion, when a new reality breaks into their sphere. The same is true of the faith that Christians bring to the world in mission. It is a commitment, not a rational certainty. It may be lost, or it may evangelize. But it is less tentative than Hoedemaker suggests, and interfaith communication is more dramatic than he portrays. The meaning of life and the hope of the world depend on the faithfulness of God whom we confess and obey. Dialogue, therefore, with those of other faiths expects a similar commitment from them. We seek common ground on matters of justice and humanity; we witness to each other in mutual respect and may modify each other's piety and even theology. And, because of that respect, we cannot but hope that they one day will covenant with the God whom we confess.

There are also idolatries. They are found in Christendom and often misuse the name of Christ; they are also in other religions, cultures, and secular enterprises. We live in the midst of their claims and must decide day by day which truth we will acknowledge and proclaim. There is no refuge, as Hoedemaker's essay shows, in sociological methods, nor in the modesty of the communicative process when it veils God's call to repentance and conversion. Modesty and self-criticism are virtues when they serve to clarify that call to us all. This theme needs to interact in the mission of the church with the dialectic of unity and diversity that Hoedemaker has so well portrayed.

Rejoinder to Charles West

As a young student, I was impressed and convinced by Charles West's approach to the problem of secularization, and by his plea to deal with that problem in a theological perspective. I am honored, therefore, by his willingness to comment on my efforts to do just that. At the same time, I am puzzled by his implicit verdict that I have gone astray.

West reads my essay as a sociological analysis. Only in the last chapter does he recognize substantial theology and explicit missionary faith. He wonders why I have "held back" so long. My essay, however, was conceived as *theological* from beginning to end. The analysis of the contemporary predicament of religion, rationality, and faith in our modern global context is not just a preface; it is part of a *theological* question. It deals with the ways in which issues of salvation, reconciliation, justice, and unity present themselves to us. H. Richard Niebuhr taught us to see the problems of faith as struggles of humankind with God. The complex field of loyalty, idolatry, enlightenment, and distortion, which we observe and seek to understand, contains judgment, challenge, and calls to conversion. This is the basic perspective of the essay. Unless they are related to an analysis of this field, our familiar and trusted words about divine revelation in Christ—including the emphasis on its otherness and beyondness—will not make any missionary sense. When revelation-speech is used to relativize and downplay the analysis of the complexity of the field of human faith and not made part of it, the missionary cause is not served but undermined. The unity of the essay is of essential importance precisely because of this.

Why is this unity not evident? Perhaps it is my "rational, instrumental" definition of faith, and my apparent inability to recognize that faith is a personal commitment to God, that moves West to say that my analysis, at least in the first five chapters, stops short of the real question and the real answer. Here, however, our difference is more a matter of appearance than of substance. Of course, faith is an existential response to God rather than loyalty to "a perspective." I do not dispute that. My point is that this response is not just an unstructured "religious" impulse (although there is some of that in faith too), but also a commitment to a community, a tradition, a story, and that this commitment structures the faith, enables its expression in words that have some coherence and some claim to rationality. Further analysis of this aspect of faith does not and should not diminish the aspect of personal commitment. But we cannot do without this further analysis: it is demanded by the problem of secularization. It is not meant to veil the reality of God's call to repentance and conversion, as West seems to think, but rather to highlight it, to interpret it, to connect it with the wider network of problems of which our repentance and conversion are a part, whether we like it or not. An explanation of what it means to respond to the living God and to the Christian gospel must receive contour and profile in the framework of an elucidation of the "eschatological" struggles of humankind. If we do not aim for something like this, our speech about faith and response will run the risk of unwittingly reproducing preoccupations of a different, bygone world experience. And then it will not be speech about the Christian gospel and will not serve its proclamation. West quotes my statement: "Revelation cannot be institutionalized as public faith; it is present in the form of an eschatological question and a challenge to reorder our configurations of religion, rationality, and faith in its perspective." That quotation should have been combined with the preceding sentence: "For me, the gospel speaks of judgment and promise, exemplified once and for all in the Christ event, and in need of recognition and reinterpretation in the tensions and conflicts of human history."

This is what mission means, in my view: introducing the force of the gospel into the complex field of global interaction with all its competing claims, idolatries, struggles for survival, and searches for truth, unity, and justice. Mission strengthens and sharpens the intuitions with regard to judgment, challenge, and calls to conversion, given the human situation. In doing so, it links those intuitions to the proclamation of a personal God and a "concrete" incarnate word. The judgment, challenge, and calls to conversion are thereby made more radical, more painful, and more personal. All that is not accomplished merely by reproducing particular interpretations of the gospel or by presenting the gospel as an alternative rationality. It is a risky hermeneutical adventure in which the meaning of the gospel itself is reconstructed through the concrete struggles of humankind. The metaphor "gathering and multiplying" is meant to indicate the basic structure of that adventure.

For West, however, this is not enough. What he finds lacking is a reference to the fact that all human dedication to unity, justice, and understanding meets its limit in the pervasiveness of sin and remains dependent on the grace of the God of the covenant. This, and only this, is the claim of Christian mission to distinctiveness. Seen from this angle, my essay describes a commendable humanistic project but not mission. Although I feel the force of this position, I do not think that it is stronger or closer to the gospel than mine. Sin and forgiveness are crucial eschatological categories. Ultimately, global human communication with all its complexities and pitfalls can only be understood in a perspective that takes these categories into account. But they need to be incarnated in our struggle for the unity of humankind, rather than presented as limit-concepts that contain some final truth "whether the world wants to know it or not." The distinctiveness of the gospel has to be tested, tried out, and subjected to reinterpretation in the arena of competing stories. That is mission.

A few minor points still remain. On the whole, many of West's remarks about rationality, religion, and faith are helpful and welcome supplements to mine. In some instances, however, I have hesitations. West's appreciation of the biblical renewal in the twentieth-century missionary movement is obviously higher than mine. As I argue in the fourth chapter, much more was needed to awaken missionary thinking to the implications of a truly global vision. The term "functional" in "functional rationality" is not used in a general way, but as a negative judgment: it is a diminished, meager rationality, from which precisely the relationality—highlighted by West—has vanished. That is the problem of secularization. One cannot simply say: rationality *is* relational—without evoking this problem and dealing with it. I have tried to deal with it in my own way by connecting rationality with its partners, religion and faith. Aside from this, I have hesitations in assuming historical continuity between faith in divine revelation, Enlightenment, Reformation, and modern functional rationality. Such assumptions were common in the earlier approaches to secularization that were indebted to people like Löwith and Gogarten. Recent analyses of the emergence of modernity (Blumenberg, Dupré) warn us against this; facile conclusions tend to gloss over the seriousness of the problem. That the term *religion* is hardly applicable to the "great faiths," that the category "does not fit," basically repeats my argument in the second chapter: the "great faiths" are complicated systems, permanently characterized by tensions between religion, rationality, and faith. My final question with regard to "religion," however, would not be "by what revealed reality is human religion brought to repentance" (West), but rather: how can we relate the Christian gospel to this complex interaction of religion and faiths, in which there is already so much judgment and challenge? At first sight, these are different questions; but are they, really?

I wonder why West does not comment on my diagnosis of secularization, on my analysis of the inadequacy of the fundamentalist response, or on the sense of urgency that characterizes the essay as a whole. Neither does he deal with the substance of my theological approach to mission. His response focuses exclusively—and, in my view, prematurely—on a supposed disagreement with regard to the nature of revelation and of faith-response. If we would have the opportunity to deal with this focus in the context of a broader and more inclusive conversation about the other issues, the supposed disagreement might lose some weight, and eventually even evaporate.

References Cited

Barth, Karl. 1936. *Church Dogmatics*. Vol. 1. Edinburgh: T. & T. Clark.

———. 1957. *Church Dogmatics*. Vol. 2:1. Edinburgh: T. & T. Clark.

Berger, Peter L. 1979. *The Heretical Imperative: Contemporary Possibilities of Religious Affirmation.* Garden City: Anchor Press.

Berger, Peter L., and Thomas Luckmann. 1966. *The Social Construction of Reality: A Sociological Treatise in the Sociology of Knowledge.* Garden City: Doubleday & Co.

Beyer, Peter. 1993. *Religion and Globalization.* London: Sage.

Cox, Harvey. 1965. *The Secular City.* New York: Macmillan & Co.

Feil, Ernst. 1986. *Religio.* Göttingen: Vandenhoeck & Ruprecht.

Habermas, Jürgen. 1981. *Theorie des Kommunikativen Handelns.* Frankfurt: Suhrkamp.

———. 1985. *Die Neue Unubersichtlichkeit.* Frankfurt: Suhrkamp.

Hadden, Jeffrey K., and Anson Shupe, eds. 1990. *Secularization and Fundamentalism Reconsidered: Religion and the Political Order.* New York: Paragon House.

Hammond, Phillip E., ed. 1985. *The Sacred in a Secular Age: Toward Revision in the Scientific Study of Religion.* Berkeley: University of California Press.

Horkheimer, Max, and Theodor Adorno. 1944. *The Dialectics of the Enlightenment.* New York: Continuum Publishing Co.

Lemaire, Ton. 1976. *Over de Waarde van Kulturen*. Baarn: Ambo.

Newbigin, Lesslie. 1978. *The Open Secret: Sketches for a Missionary Theology*. Grand Rapids: Eerdmans.

———. 1983. *The Other Side of 1984*. Geneva: WCC Publications.

———. 1986. *Foolishness to the Greeks: The Gospel and Western Culture*. Grand Rapids: Eerdmans.

———. 1989. *The Gospel in a Pluralist Society*. Grand Rapids: Eerdmans.

———. 1991. *Truth to Tell: The Gospel as Public Truth*. Grand Rapids: Eerdmans.

Niebuhr, Reinhold. 1943. *The Nature and Destiny of Man*. Vol. 2. New York: Scribners.

Pannenberg, Wolfhart. 1989. *Christianity in a Secularized World*. London: SCM Press.

Raiser, Konrad. 1991. *Ecumenism in Transition: A Paradigm Shift in the Ecumenical Movement*. Geneva: WCC Publications.

Robertson, Roland. 1985. *The Sacred and the World System*, in Hammond, ed., 347–58.

———. 1990. *A New Perspective on Religion and Secularization*, in Hadden and Shupe, eds., 63–77.

Smith, Wilfred Cantwell. 1964. *The Meaning and End of Religion*. New York: Mentor Books.

———. 1981. *Towards a World Theology*. Philadelphia: Westminster Press.

Toulmin, Stephen. 1990. *Cosmopolis: The Hidden Agenda of Modernity*. Chicago: University of Chicago Press.

Tracy, David. 1987. *Plurality and Ambiguity: Hermeneutics, Religion, Hope*. London: SCM Press.

van Leeuwen, Arend T. 1964. Trans. by H. H. Hoskins. *Christianity in World History*. New York: Scribners.

Vroom, H. M. 1989. *Religions and the Truth: Philosophical Reflections and Perspectives*. Trans. by J. W. Rebel. Amsterdam: Editions Rodopi/Grand Rapids: Eerdmans.